M000169505

Brian Bennett is a l... understands the hea... addition, he loves p... "gracist"!

—DAVID ANDERSON, founder and senior pastor of
Bridgeway Community Church

This book will show you a beautiful picture of what it looks like to journey together daily. Bennett shares his experience of bridging gaps between cultures, while helping us discover what kingdom life looks like wherever we are. *Go Now and Be the Church* will move people into action in caring for their communities through listening, patience, and reconciliation.

—CHARLES ARN, author of *Side Door* (WPH) and
professor of outreach at Wesley Seminary

In a time when we in America still struggle with how to be a diverse group of people and live in unity, Brian Bennett's book is a must-read for anyone interested in how the church can be an agent of reconciliation and service in the community. Bennett not only is the key leader and pastor of Overflow Church, but he also tells Overflow Church's story in a marvelous and compelling manner that will entertain, inform, and inspire.

—TONY CAMPBELL, director of missional engagement and
global mission for the Reformed Church in America

Brian Bennett takes the time to share with us his journey (most inspiring) and helps us understand how the church the Lord led him to plant has become a model of a church that has the potential to change the world. The principles Bennett presents are transferable and will work in different situations. Bennett shares from his heart nuggets of truth that helped him go from rented space to a thriving soon-to-be-multisite congregation.

—ANTHONY M. GRAHAM, senior pastor of New Hope Family Worship Center

With candor and humility, Bennett takes us on a spiritual roller-coaster ride through a real-life kingdom adventure. This wisdom-packed book reveals how the life of faith is anything but stress-free, yet exciting beyond belief. *Go Now and Be the Church* is an inspiring and instructive account of urban community transformation and the transformation of a leader called to serve.

—BOB LUPTON, founder and president of FCS Urban Ministries

Through real experience, Brian Bennett shows us what it looks like to actively pursue a multicultural community by living out the Great Commission. *Go Now and Be the Church* can and will bring transformation to those who read it seeking a true understanding of discipleship of all peoples.

—JO ANNE LYON, general superintendent of The Wesleyan Church

A refreshing format and faith-building content makes *Go Now and Be the Church* a true spiritual adventure. Having followed Brian's ministry since the founding of Overflow Church, the perspectives he shares arise out of effective service to a people and a place he loves.

—WAYNE SCHMIDT, author of *Ministry Velocity* (WPH)
and vice president of Wesley Seminary

Get ready to take a journey that is both fresh and profoundly helpful. Through Scripture, powerful story, and beautiful reflection, Brian challenges Christians everywhere to engage in the call to go and be the church—now!

—JEREMY SUMMERS, author, pastor, and director of
adult spiritual formation for The Wesleyan Church

Go Now and Be the CHURCH

Becoming an Overflowing Community

Brian D. Bennett

wesleyan
PUBLISHING HOUSE
wphstore.com

Copyright © 2016 by Brian Bennett
Published by Wesleyan Publishing House
Indianapolis, Indiana 46250
Printed in the United States of America
ISBN: 978-1-63257-089-5
ISBN (e-book): 978-1-63257-090-1

Library of Congress Cataloging-in-Publication Data

Bennett, Brian (Pastor)
  Go now and be the church : becoming an overflowing community / Brian Bennett.
Indianapolis : Wesleyan Publishing House, 2016.
LCCN 2015036880 | ISBN 9781632570895 (pbk.)
LCSH: Church. | Wesleyan Church--Doctrines.
LCC BV600.3 .B463 2016 | DDC 253--dc23 LC record available at
http://lccn.loc.gov/2015036880

Cover design: Cody Rayn

Go Now and Be the Church is dedicated to the people of Overflow Church in Benton Harbor, Michigan. Thank you for faithfully living out, every week, what it means to passionately follow Jesus and joyfully serve others. May we continue to go now and be the church and share his story for his glory.

Contents

For additional free resources, visit
wphresources.com/gonow.

Acknowledgements

This book would not be possible without the blessing of my best friend, wife, and co-laborer in the gospel, Cindy Bennett. She has faithfully served to help plant and lead Overflow Church alongside me and has stood by my side as I have worked on this project for the past few years. I also want to thank my mother, Debbie Bennett, for the many hours she spent praying, editing, and encouraging me during the writing process.

Introduction

It is amazing how God works in and through some of life's most difficult seasons to bring great clarity and beauty. In the fall of 2011, I had reached a place of burnout in life, leadership, and ministry. During this time, leaders in my denomination provided a church planter renewal grant that allowed me and my family to pursue renewal and healing. We took a family vacation; my wife, Cindy, and I had time away as a couple; and I visited a retreat center for counseling, solitude, and silence. Until then, the heavy demands and financial constraints of planting a church and starting a nonprofit had not afforded us these much-needed breaks. During my time at the retreat center, I was able to get back to the core of who I am in Christ, who Christ is in his church, and what I believe it means to be the people of God and live as his church. I cannot recall exactly how it happened or what triggered the thought process, but in my journal from September 23 of that year I wrote this: "Overflow benediction each week? 'Go now and be the church—salt and light.'"

In that moment the idea for a weekly benediction at Overflow Church came together. Our benediction became, and remains to this day, "May you journey together this week, learning to passionately follow Jesus and joyfully serve others. Go now and be the church." It is both a blessing and a commissioning, a time the congregation has grown to love and see as a rally cry at the close of each service. We don't just gather to *do* church; we are given the opportunity to *be* the church in our community. We have faithfully lived out this concept since I returned from that retreat. However, the heart, vision, and passion behind that expression actually began four years earlier in 2007 when Overflow Church was in its early stages. The concept of being the church in our community, of taking Jesus beyond our walls and seeing life transformation in our region, has always been with us. Though we did not verbalize that benediction in the first few years, we were living it out as witnesses to our community.

Throughout this journey, you will find stories from the formational years of Overflow Church and daily devotions to encourage and equip you. The reflection questions will help you apply what you are learning to your ministry context. My prayer and hope is that you will renew your walk with Christ, your walk with his church, and embrace the call to go now and be the church in your community.

PART 1

Discovering Kingdom Life

Not that I speak in regard to need, for I have learned in whatever state I am, to be content: I know how to be abased, and I know how to abound. Everywhere and in all things I have learned both to be full and to be hungry, both to abound and to suffer need. I can do all things through Christ who strengthens me.

—Philippians 4:11–13 NKJV

1

Contentment and Holy Discontent

I am a discontented person by nature. Some part of me has always tried to look ahead to what's next more than to enjoy what is now. In 2005 I left my first career as an inner-city public school teacher and coach to join the staff of a two-thousand-person church as a youth and young adult pastor. I strongly believed God had called me to that ministry, and I was excited to dive in. I found myself in my midtwenties with a great ministry position, working toward a master's degree, with a wonderful wife and our first child. I was living the dream, finding a season of true contentment, or so I thought.

However, within a few months my wife began to sense a significant discontentment growing within her. As she shared it with me, I told her it was too soon to make a judgment about our current situation and that she should pray through it to find contentment. It did not take long, though, for that feeling of discontent to affect me as well. We were experiencing a godly discontent. God was moving in our lives, and I was simply slow to respond. The discontentment stemmed from my sense of being called to build bridges between people and God. I had developed such a heart for diversity and the poor from my time in the inner-city schools that I knew our lives and ministry had to include this focus. The setting I was in, though not resistant to that, was not intentionally seeking diversity. I discovered then the difference between ministries focused on attracting people (drawing people to them) and those focused on reaching people (connecting with people in the midst of their daily lives and activities). Above all, I knew my life had to be about a kingdom-building ministry that would extend beyond the church walls to embrace the city and region where I found myself, one that reflected the aspect of Jesus' ministry that most resonated with me.

During that season, Jeremiah 29:7 began to burn within me during my devotional times, calling Cindy and me to something more. This powerful verse says, "Also, seek the peace and prosperity of the city to which I have carried you into exile. Pray to the LORD for it, because if it prospers, you too will prosper." My godly discontent drove me to leave what I thought was everything for something more, and I found that something was the everything I had been looking for all along.

There is a difference, however, between godly discontent and what I would call personal discontent. The former is driven by God and relates to our callings; the latter stems from frustration with personal circumstances. Personal contentment is one of the chief Christian virtues. The apostle Paul learned the secret of contentment in Jesus Christ. As followers of Jesus, we are encouraged to be content with our God and all that he has supplied us with. This virtue of contentment may be considered a vice by the world around us, but it is one of the core characteristics of a walk with Jesus. In a world that constantly encourages us to make comparisons, to want more, to be more, and to do more, only Christ's strength enables us to find contentment.

However, beyond the question of personal contentment with the circumstances of our lives lies the question of where God may, in fact, be moving us to change or grow. Often God will give us a burden or a state of discontent with the present to lead us toward the next step he has for our lives. We may at first interpret this as dissatisfaction or frustration with our circumstances, but it may be something more. What begins as a feeling of dissatisfaction or frustration, if directed by God, can become the fuel that propels us toward the next season of life or ministry. It was a godly discontent that moved us to launch out and start what would become Overflow Church. This godly discontent was affirmed by Jeremiah 29:7. The question of what it would look like see God's holistic healing and peace take place in a community began to burn within me. After months of wrestling with this Scripture and bathing it in prayer, the next steps, as directed by God, began to emerge, leading us an entirely new direction in life and ministry.

Discussion Questions

1. Would you describe yourself as very discontent, somewhat discontent, somewhat content, or very content? If on the discontent side of the scale, is it personal or godly discontent? Explain what you mean.

2. In the areas of life where you are discontent, do you sense that it is driven by comparisons to others? What seems to drive your discontent most of the time?

3. What disciplines or habits help you experience contentment?

4. How does your understanding of Philippians 4:13, "I can do all things through Christ who strengthens me"

(NKJV), change when you read it in its context of being content in life?

5. If you have any godly discontent in life right now, what vision for change might God be birthing in you?

6. Nehemiah took his godly discontent before God in prayer (see Neh. 1), which led to his vision for rebuilding Jerusalem's walls. How might you pray over your feeling of discontent so that God can work within you?

And afterward, I will pour out my Spirit on all people. Your sons and daughters will prophesy, your old men will dream dreams, your young men will see visions.

—Joel 2:28

2

Dreams and Visions

The conversation with our senior pastor, my boss, was one I will never forget. He was humble and wise in advising me to pray over our discontentment to discern whether it was merely personal or a prompting from God. During that conversation, he talked both about future ministry possibilities at that church and about exploring the option of church planting by attending a church planter assessment. I had sensed a calling to plant a church, and now it seemed like right time to explore it. Cindy and I attended the assessment together. It was an intense four-day period.

We were under a high level of scrutiny, but our passion for the idea of planting was also rising. By the end of those four days, we knew we were called to plant a church and the time for that would be coming soon. On our last evening at the assessment center, Cindy and I compared notes that we'd each jotted on napkins, notes in which we'd independently ranked the handful of job offers I had, including the idea of planting a church. We had both moved church planting from dead last to first. I shared with her my growing burden for Southwest Michigan, even though we had only driven through the area. As Cindy shared her thoughts on Benton Harbor and St. Joseph, we looked at the demographics online and realized we had found the community God had been preparing us for.

Benton Harbor and St. Joseph, Michigan, were referred to lovingly as the "twin cities" in decades past but have stood deeply divided for the past thirty years. Separated by the St. Joseph River, the two communities are a sharp contrast: the St. Joseph population consists of over 90 percent Caucasians with a median income higher than the state average; just across the river is Benton Harbor, which is over 90 percent African American and has a median income below the poverty line. Given the economic and racial polarization of these two communities over the decades, we knew this was precisely where God wanted us to spend our lives seeking "the peace and prosperity of the city" (Jer. 29:7).

With great excitement we prayed together over the communities of Benton Harbor and St. Joseph, resolving to answer God's call. That same night, Cindy had a dream and vision regarding the community. Here is a portion of that dream as she'd recounted it in her diary:

February 28, 2007: I had a dream last night. I saw a mall, a stage, a community center, and a Jo-Ann Fabrics store in my dream, with all people, a multicultural community, coming together in worship. I woke up and began praying for this region, asking the Lord to soften hearts and break strongholds. I prayed so loudly that I woke up Brian. In his "love your wife as Christ loves the church" voice, he asked me what I was doing up at 3:00 a.m. After telling him, he shared in my excitement! We knew God was calling us to plant a church. We now had our answer for the assessment team. I had another dream that included a beach and driving over a bridge to a neighboring town. Today, Brian and I share a burden for the St. Joseph/Benton Harbor area. These are adjacent beach cities separated by a bridge.

God had spoken in many ways and now confirmed his direction through a unique and clear dream and vision. The fact that our God desires to work in and through his people is astounding. The One who created the universe in all its expansiveness also reaches out to us individually, inviting us into relationship with him and into his work in our world. God began his invitation into his work through a godly discontent. This call was affirmed through other believers and finally confirmed through a unique dream and vision. According to Joel 2:28, visions are a way that God speaks to his people. Though this experience was a first for Cindy and me, that vision would serve as the pivotal and confirming moment in the journey to follow God's plan and start Overflow Church.

When you consider how God may be speaking to you, it's important to understand that dreams and visions could be a part of the plan but are an exception to the rule and not God's most common way to communicate. As Henry Blackaby noted, God will speak to us through four primary means: through the Bible, through prayer and worship, through the church (other believers), and through circumstances.[1] As you seek God's direction for your life, check every decision through the lens of these four methods. Begin by asking yourself what the Bible has to say about that direction and situation. Consider what God is saying to you as you pray and worship him. As you seek wise counsel from other believers or hear from pastoral leaders in church, consider if their wisdom aligns with the direction you feel God is leading. And last, think about whether the circumstances of your life seem to point in the direction you are considering. This last question is very important in this day when people often take an "open door" as a sign of God's will. Though you may have an opportunity in front of you, it is vitally important to check your decision through the other ways in which God communicates. Otherwise, you may stumble through an open door that is merely a distraction. For Cindy and me, it was the alignment of all four of God's primary methods of speaking, together with Cindy's dream and vision, that convinced us it was time to move forward.

Discussion Questions

1. How does it make you feel to realize that God, in all his greatness, desires to know you and work in and through you?

2. Have you ever had a dream or vision that you felt was from God? What was it? What did you do after that dream or vision, and how has it affected your life since?

3. As you reflect on your life and walk with God, what do you notice about the ways he speaks to you?

4. As you review Henry Blackaby's paradigm of the four primary methods through which God speaks, which one seems to be most common for you? Which one could you explore more fully?

5. What would change in your life or ministry if you took more seriously the idea that all four of the primary methods through which God speaks should be in alignment before you make a major decision?

Note

1. Henry T. Blackaby and Claude V. King, *Experiencing God: Knowing and Doing the Will of God*, workbook (Nashville: LifeWay, 1990), 83.

3

Power and Provision in Prayer

Experiencing a true dream and vision from the Lord in the middle of the night, coupled with our clear sense of calling to Benton Harbor and St. Joseph, Michigan, led Cindy and me to passionate prayer. We realized the magnitude of what God was calling us to within two communities that were deeply divided. As our time spent in prayer began to grow, the fire within us burned ever brighter. We began with drive-by prayer, driving around the community, looking, listening, and praying. We were looking to see where God was already at work in hopes of joining him there. During these prayer times, God shaped our vision, filled our hearts, and directed our steps.

Our initial visit to Orchards Mall occurred within a week of Cindy's dream and vision. All of the key elements in her dream were present in the mall, and we knew God was up to something significant. We prayed on the spot and then had a conversation with the mall manager, who later would provide a favorable lease for our first office and prayer event in the mall. We realized that God was way ahead of us and was showing us that prayer must precede our every step if we were to see his power and provision.

On September 23, 2007, we held our first public event in the mall community center. We gathered with more than eighty people to praise God, then broke into three groups to drive across the three bridges between Benton Harbor and St. Joseph, asking God to turn them from dividers into connectors. We experienced a few glitches that evening, but the spirit of faith and prayer was strong. During this event my dad walked the adjacent Sears property (due to its close proximity to our even location), pushing my then six-month-old son in a stroller in circle after circle around the store, praying for our new ministry. When that same property was donated to our church three years later, we realized the connection between those circles of prayer and God's provision in our ministry. True power comes only through seeking God's help, through our prayers.

Prayer is a mystery, yet it stands out as one of the primary characteristics of Jesus' life and ministry. Jesus modeled a powerful prayer life that was consistent, constant, and much like the act of breathing. Prayer should be like breathing in the life of the believer, and like a pillar on which we lean for God's wisdom and power. The ministry of prayer has been central to the work God called us to in Benton Harbor.

As you consider Jesus' words in Mark 9:29, remember that the context was a powerful moment of life change in which he healed a boy that others could not. What was the difference between Jesus' approach and that of his disciples? It was his reliance on prayer and fasting. Author Philip Yancey said, "If prayer stands as the place where God and human beings meet, then I must learn about prayer. Most of my struggles in the Christian life circle around the same two themes: why God doesn't act the way we want God to, and why I don't act the way God wants me to. Prayer is the precise point where those themes converge."[1]

Prayer should be as natural as breathing and will help you align yourself with God and his will for your life. Overflow Church is 100 percent committed to prayer and fasting as a central part of its life and ministry. We can attest to the power that comes from prayer to accomplish

God's will in our world. Maybe it is time for you to raise the temperature of prayer in your life and begin all of your initiatives with prayer and fasting. Are you ready to see what God will do to transform your life through the power of prayer? We pray that you are inspired to dive in and take your prayer life to another level today, tomorrow, and for the future.

Discussion Questions

1. How would you describe your prayer life: ice cold, cool, lukewarm, hot, or on fire? Explain what you mean.

2. What aspect of prayer and fasting excites you, and what concerns you?

3. Does Philip Yancey's statement that prayer is the point at which his two primary struggles converge encourage or challenge you? Why?

4. For what and whom could you pray today to take your prayer life to another level?

5. In Colossians 1:9–11, the apostle Paul prayed that believers may be filled with God, may be faithful to God, and may be fruitful for God. Pray those verses for someone in your life today.

Note

1. Philip Yancey, *Prayer: Does It Make Any Difference?* (Grand Rapids, MI: Zondervan, 2006), 17.

Then a certain scribe came and said to Him, "Teacher, I will follow You wherever You go." And Jesus said to him, "Foxes have holes and birds of the air have nests, but the Son of Man has nowhere to lay His head." Then another of His disciples said to Him, "Lord, let me first go and bury my father." But Jesus said to him, "Follow Me, and let the dead bury their own dead."

—Matthew 8:19–22 NKJV

4

Burning Bridges and Following Jesus

To a church that is radically focused on building bridges, the notion of burning bridges sounds foreign, almost offensive. For Christ-followers, though, there are moments in our lives when we know that burning a bridge is exactly what we must do to be faithful to Jesus. During the first few months of answering the call to plant Overflow Church, it became clear that we would be faced with many challenges financially, both as a family and as a new church plant. Having very little financial support and almost no prospects on the horizon, I began to pray—and panic. I have found that the space between prayer and panic is where God reveals himself and grows my faith the most.

In my panic I began to apply for teaching jobs in our new community and even applied for one position two hours away. You can likely guess what happened. I received a job offer to teach and coach in a school two hours from the community I knew God had called us to. A way to provide for my family, which now included two children under age three, was now in front of me. Missing, however, was the sense of Jesus saying, "Follow me." In fact, I felt that Jesus was telling me to "burn the bridge" and follow him to Benton Harbor and St. Joseph. It was a moment of truth. After wrestling with this decision in prayer, I called the principal to explain that I was humbled by their offer but certain they wanted someone who would be there for more than one year, and I could not commit to that. By burning that bridge, I felt a greater sense of fulfillment and freedom to follow Jesus into the adventure he had planned.

That adventure would include an incredible amount of "friend raising" as God began to open doors and build new bridges to people who would pray for us, network for us, volunteer with us, and financially contribute to us. We spoke in forty churches over eighteen months to raise support, and God faithfully built new bridges to people we still call friends. By following God to our new community, and not taking a job miles away, I had the time to network in the community and beyond. These new relational bridges may never have formed if the first bridges hadn't been burned by faith.

The call to follow Jesus is the essence of the Christian life. We are not just saved from our sins; we are brought into a new and abundant life that we discover as we follow Jesus, one day and one decision at a time. Often, that means making changes and leaving things behind to move forward with God. As we follow him and let go of the things that may hold us back, we find that God builds new bridges that lead to his best for us. In Overflow's story there have been moments that required burning bridges in order to follow Jesus, which has required ever-deeper levels of trust and a willingness to believe that God's plan would unfold in a new way as he builds bridges to the future he has designed.

In Matthew 8, Jesus described the cost of following him, stating that the "Son of Man has nowhere to lay His head (v. 20 NKJV)." Jesus was teaching his disciples that to follow him was to trust him for everything. When just a few moments later Jesus told a man whose father had just died to "let the dead bury their own dead" (v. 22 NKJV) and follow him, it seems harsh. However, it appears that Jesus was speaking to the issue of timing. The delay in following could have been months or even years as the man mourned the death and settled his father's estate. Jesus would accept no such delay.

There are a multitude of reasons to delay in following Jesus, but they pale in comparison to the life of adventure you will experience as you journey forward with him. Consider the cost of following him, but realize the opportunity and reward you will gain by seeing Jesus work in his time and in his way to provide for you. The adventure lies before you, and I pray you will move forward today.

Discussion Questions

1. When you read the first two sentences of today's devotional, what was your immediate reaction?

2. How would you describe the difference between being saved by Jesus and being his follower?

3. There is a difference between being a fan of Jesus and being a follower of Jesus. Which would you say you are? Explain what you mean.

4. What bridges may you need to burn in order to move forward and follow Jesus?

5. The verses from Mathew 8 show that God's provision and timing are central areas in which we must trust him. Which one of these is your greatest struggle? Why?

6. How have you noticed God building bridges to the future in your life?

"Ask, and it will be given to you; seek, and you will find; knock, and it will be opened to you. For everyone who asks receives, and he who seeks finds, and to him who knocks it will be opened. . . . If you then, being evil, know how to give good gifts to your children, how much more will your Father who is in heaven give good things to those who ask Him!"

—Matthew 7:7–8, 11 NKJV

5

God's Miraculous Provision

Maybe you have heard of situations in which people have received miraculous provision and thought, "I would love to have that happen to me." I think we all would love to see a miracle in our lives, but we don't want to embrace the situations that become the context for a miracle. In the first few months after leaving my role as a youth and young adult pastor, Cindy and I went through a season of extremes. One day would bring courage, and the next would bring doubt. One moment would bring encouragement, the next despair. Through this experience, God laid the foundation of faith for his miraculous provision, which began one Thursday around the kitchen table.

Cindy and I had been praying, planning, and working on reaching out to our new community and to people who might partner with us. We hadn't witnessed much result for our efforts, and this particular week had run our bank account completely empty. Cindy showed me a bill for fifteen hundred dollars that was due the next day, and we both felt overwhelmed. We did the only thing we knew to do: We turned to God. Cindy and I sat around the kitchen table and prayerfully laid our financial need before God, asking for his provision. True to his promises, God provided for our need the very next day. Friday morning I went to the mailbox, and there was a donation check to our ministry for exactly fifteen hundred dollars! God miraculously provided, and we experienced it because we were willing to follow him into situations that only he could solve.

That check we received in the mail has paid immeasurable spiritual dividends in the years since. It planted seeds of faith deep within our hearts that even today help us trust God in new ways. We have found over and over again that where God guides, he provides. The answered prayer and provision that Friday started a seedling of support that grew in the months and years ahead as God brought us equipment, donations, volunteers, leaders, transportation, and a building. We learned then, and believe now, that there will always be a God-sized gap in any plan that is truly from him, and it's in that gap that his miraculous provision comes through.

Have you ever read in a missionary's biography or heard from a pastor a powerful story of God's miraculous provision? These inspirational stories increase our faith and lead us to celebrate God's care for his people. You may wonder if that is something God will do for you or if those miracles are just for others. Matthew 7 teaches us that God wants us to ask, seek, and knock regarding our needs. God is a good Father who desires to give us good gifts! What a powerful truth that is, and one that shows God is willing to miraculously provide for each of us as we have need.

As we faced an early, and significant, financial challenge, Cindy and I realized we had nowhere else to turn. We simply turned to God in prayer at the kitchen table, seeking direction and knocking on the storehouse of heaven for God's good gifts. At the time, we had only heard and read about stories of miraculous provision. Now we have experienced it firsthand. Our God is able to provide, as we trust him.

God has a story to write in your life, and the very places you have gaps and needs are the places in which he will show up miraculously, proving himself to be the giver of good gifts. May you take your needs to him in prayer today and see his miraculous provision!

Discussion Questions

1. What stories of miraculous provision have you experienced or heard about? Reflect on these and encourage yourself or one another.

2. How would you describe the difference between needs and wants?

3. When we follow Jesus we may find there are more gaps and needs than we are used to. What does this tell us about the place of faith and prayer in following Jesus?

4. In a practical sense, what would it mean for us to follow Jesus' instruction to ask, seek, and knock?

5. When you have a significant need, what is your first response: prayer, worry, work, wallowing, or something else?

6. Do you trust that God is a good Father who desires to give good gifts to his children? If not, why not? If so, how does that belief show itself in your life?

7. What needs will you present to God today, asking for his miraculous provision?

PART 2

Modern-Day Wells

But someone will say, "You have faith, and I have works." Show me your faith without your works, and I will show you my faith by my works.

—James 2:18 NKJV

6

Faith Works

As the journey to plant Overflow Church began, Cindy and I felt excitement and great anticipation of what God would do. We envisioned a church that would truly be a place of hope and healing. We envisioned Jesus satisfying people's thirst at this modern-day "well" just as he did for the Samaritan woman two thousand years ago (see John 4). One early goal was to find a space in our community that would facilitate this vision. Our dream was to use commercial spaces, to be in the marketplace. But that required resources we did not have.

Within this tension of dreams versus reality, we began to see faith work. Faith comes from God, and, when we are led by God, faith accomplishes his purpose. With no training or background in fund-raising, we began to pray and work. We started by sending a mailing to over four hundred ministries and individuals across the country. Every letter was followed up with a personal e-mail, a phone call, and the hope of sharing what God had laid on our hearts for Benton Harbor and St. Joseph. I wish I could say that every contact was a success. It wasn't. But I can say that our faith was put to work during this season and that it bore fruit. As we walked faithfully, we found that God would open doors to new prayer partners, friends, donations, mentors, volunteers, and anything else we needed. In addition, what didn't help grow the ministry directly grew us instead. Every yes opened a door to ministry, and every no opened a door to greater faith.

As doors opened for sharing our vision with others, we found ourselves traveling many miles, sharing many meals, and speaking many times with churches of all sizes. We spoke in churches ranging in size from eighteen people to three thousand people. Cindy and our two little children traveled with me every weekend, and grandparents often joined us to help with the kids while we met with people. Cindy created all our printed materials herself. Though she has no formal training, the results were so good that someone once asked who our graphic designer was and if they would be able to use that person too. God gave us wisdom and gifts beyond what we knew we possessed for this journey. Regardless of the size of the group or our perception of the opportunity, we trusted God and went. During that first year, I put more than forty thousand miles on my 2003 Hyundai Accent. That little car worked hard, and so did we. I felt as if we were seeing the seeds of destiny that God had planted in my heart four years earlier coming to fruition.

Here is a journal entry I wrote in 2003, four years before we planted Overflow Church:

Lord, show us what we should labor for, what culture we are to commit to in order that the Word is given to others. My burden for the city has grown into a vision for [church planting]—I am scared and really feel foolish to dream so big—to have a vision (to plant a church) that affects a city, a country, and a world . . . a springboard for change, a vehicle for the gospel, and advance for the kingdom. My heart's desire is to pursue you and know your heart.

We learned during this season that God not only will provide miraculously but will also direct our steps to the right people and places if we put our faith to work. This season required a tremendous amount of work, yet we found that God's grace was not just sufficient for our need; it was overflowing.

We sometimes talk about stepping out in faith as if that is the one and only step necessary in walking with God into the future he has for us. That initial step is only the first in a long journey that will require many steps of faith. As the apostle James stated, "Show me your faith without your works, and I will show you my faith by my works" (1:18 NKJV). As we walk by faith, we begin to operate from a place of faith. In the Overflow story, there was a tremendous amount of driving, speaking, networking, writing, calling, mailing, and many other tasks required to share the vision and gather support. There were also many moments of weariness. Yet all of it was touched by God's hand through the faith that was at work in us.

Consider your life and the things you hope for. If you believe God is leading you to step out in faith, you must also consider the role of work in that journey. Any work we do for Christ is possible only through him (see John 15:5). Your role is to be the empty vessel for him to work through (see 2 Cor. 4:7). Yet, when you begin to trust God deeply, you will be willing to roll up your sleeves and work alongside him in what he is doing. God is already at work and gives you the joy-filled privilege of taking part in what he is doing. It is humbling and a great honor to realize that God wants our participation. When we let go and let God use us in greater ways, he blesses our work. "His story, his glory" is a theme of Overflow Church, and during those early days we saw that theme become reality.

Not every letter was answered, not every person decided to participate in the Overflow story, and not every call or e-mail was returned. But some were. It was in the "some" that God's hand and blessing were revealed through faith that works.

Discussion Questions

1. How do you understand the relationship between faith and works in the life of a believer?

2. In general, have you been someone who was more driven by faith or by the work of ministry? Explain.

3. Faith produces action on the part of the faith-filled person, and as we abide in Christ (see John 15:5) we can expect fruit to follow. In what ways have you been willing to put your faith into action and do the work?

4. In what area do you sense God calling you to step out in faith?

5. As you step out in faith, what kind of work will be required? How will you prepare yourself for what that will mean?

6. What steps can you take this week to put your faith to work and begin making a difference in the world around you?

7. Reflect on the idea that God is already at work with you and will produce a result if you say yes to him.

Strengthen the feeble hands, steady the knees that give way; say to those with fearful hearts, "Be strong, do not fear; your God will come, he will come with vengeance; with divine retribution he will come to save you."

—Isaiah 35:3–4

7

Moving Forward with Fear in the Rear

You cannot drive a car forward by looking in the rearview mirror. To move ahead you must look through the windshield. As Cindy and I moved forward in faith to begin Overflow Church, many fears surfaced. Each time a fear popped up, I found myself looking in the rearview mirror and wondering if we had made the right decision. I questioned whether God would come through and doubted the future. It was an intense time of soul searching and one in which I learned an important lesson: I needed to put fear in the rear not in the future.

During this season, I clung to God and found my faith and hope growing through an intense study of the book of

Isaiah and a book called *Chasing Daylight* by Erwin McManus. I learned that desperation could create either despair or dependence on God, and I chose deeper dependence. That dependence drove us forward. As McManus said, "The door we fear going through the most may be the very one where we will meet God most profoundly."[1] God led us a step at a time through the fears and into a deeper faith, a more dangerous faith.

This dangerous faith sustained me through six weeks of wrestling with fear. My fears took the shape of questions ranging from "Is this really God calling us?" to "How will we feed our young family?" and "Who will want to be a part of this church anyway?" These fears were like onslaughts of fiery arrows aimed at my mind and heart. They seemed to overwhelm me at times. I remember days when I just needed the faith to get through the next fifteen minutes. As God helped me overcome fear, my faith grew stronger moment by moment. Putting fear in the rear, we moved forward and continued to see victory after victory. I wish someone had told me then that this struggle to move forward despite fear was a central part of God's plan to develop me and our future church. David learned this by facing a lion and a bear in preparation for his battle with Goliath and his future reign as king (see 1 Sam. 17). Everyone who wants to move forward with God must overcome fear through faith.

Perhaps you have experienced the way fear works against forward progress in life. Fear, unless it is the fear (or reverence) of God, is one of the Enemy's most effective weapons. Fear will crouch at the door of your heart, circle around you throughout the day, and cloud your mind with a fog of lies and deception. Fear will harass you in moments of decision. It will work overtime to prevent you from experiencing the victory that can be yours when you move forward in faith. The Enemy seeks to sabotage Christ's mission, and you are part of that mission.

This is why Jesus spent every spare moment with his Father, gaining strength for the next challenge. When facing fear, you will find that your times with God must go deeper, further, and longer than they have ever gone before. To make the journey with Christ into his work, you must be strengthened and equipped in him constantly. He is the only source for the faith that overcomes fear.

Erwin McManus said, "You cannot follow God in neutral. God has created you to do something."[2] Has fear held you in neutral? Perhaps it is the fear of failure and God is asking you to learn from your failures and walk forward with him. Maybe it is the fear of disapproval, and God is asking you to work for no one but him. Whatever your fears may be, face them. Dig deeper into your walk with God, and you will have the faith to overcome. For me, time spent in the book of Isaiah brought the inspiration and encouragement that led to forward progress. It may be time for you to dig into the Bible and ask God to encourage you in the areas in which you fear so you can more closely follow his call on your life. Do not stay stuck in neutral. God is dynamic and on the move in our world. Let him draw you, challenge you, encourage you, fill you, and move you forward in life.

Discussion Questions

1. What are your greatest fears? Where did these come from?

2. What role has fear played in your life over the years, either positive or negative? How has it impacted your decision making?

3. When you consider the statement "We cannot follow God in neutral," what comes to mind? What gear are you currently in: reverse, neutral, first, second, third, fourth?

4. Is there one particular area in which you are stuck in neutral? What do you think God would say to you about the fear that is holding you back?

5. What would help you move to the next gear and achieve greater forward progress in your walk with God?

6. Which book of the Bible has had the biggest impact on you? Why?

7. What is your next step? Take it to God in prayer, asking for victory over fear.

Notes

1. Erwin McManus, *Chasing Daylight: Seize the Power of Every Moment* (Nashville: Thomas Nelson, 2002), 101.

2. Ibid., 36.

8

Little Is Big with God

Everyone loves a story of humble beginnings. We tout the rags-to-riches hero or the from-ashes-to-beauty heroine and celebrate their successes. What happens, though, when you move from big to little and must redefine everything about your life in order to see what God is doing? That is exactly what happened to our family as we left a church of more than two thousand in weekly attendance to start Overflow Church with just six people—including Cindy and me. This transition was humbling but necessary. It was necessary to begin small so we could see God at work in the myriad of little things he was doing—some of which were really quite big!

Our outreach ministry began by starting a Bible study, which we held in a storefront office in a mall, and a weekly kids' program we led at the community center of a housing project. During this season, we reached many people (meeting practical needs, building friends, and even baptizing some) with Jesus' love and we, too, were transformed by Jesus. Often what seems little in our eyes is quite big in God's sight. We may recognize this only in retrospect. One of my favorite memories of this time is the way God allowed our small, 700-square-foot storefront to become a place of peace and refuge for mall employees and mall walkers. One day a store manager fell asleep on our couch and said it was the best rest she'd had in a long time.

During that humble beginning, we saw five people baptized (in a health club swimming pool), many relationships formed, and the creation of a launch team for our first public service. God moved in and through these seemingly little activities began to fashion his very big future for Overflow Church. He had allowed us to be truly ordinary at the start so that when he began to do extraordinary things it would be clear that it was his doing and not ours. The extraordinary events that followed would include the donation of a 130,000-square-foot building, the start-up of a nonprofit focused on community development, and the baptism of many believers at Overflow Church over the years (more than 260 at the time of this writing). Little truly is big with our God.

Overflow Church's small beginning continues to shape our ministry in ways that keep it focused on Christ and people. Cindy and I had to go through a major shift in our understanding of what really matters as we left a very large ministry to start small with Overflow Church. Through the process, I found myself at times frustrated, discouraged, and even insecure. Yet God was both transforming me and preparing the church for an extraordinary future.

What seemingly small things has God entrusted to you? Have you considered how vastly different are the ways of God's kingdom and those of the world? It is clear throughout Scripture that we are not to despise small beginnings and to be faithful with little so that we may be given more. Jesus taught that the kingdom is like a mustard seed in that it begins small, smaller than almost anything else, yet it grows to become one of the largest plants (see Matt. 13:31–32). It can often be easy to dismiss this truth because it is familiar. However, just for a moment, let it sink into your soul. Try to absorb the revolutionary idea that little is big with our God! Any number of things in your life may seem small and insignificant; yet with God's hand and blessing, they can be extraordinary if only you are faithful.

In this twenty-first-century culture that likes to see instant results, we must look to Jesus and realize that his ways often take a different shape—an unexpected form—and take place on a longer timeline. According to Zechariah, we should not look at the small amount done today but at what is possible in the future with God's hand on the work (see Zech. 4:10). Also through this prophet God told us that it is "not by might nor by power, but by [his] Spirit" that victory will come (4:6 NKJV). Be encouraged that with God's Spirit empowering your work, the future will be extraordinary as you stay faithful.

Discussion Questions

1. Have you ever started a project and not finished it? If so, what kept you from finishing the project?

2. Can you think of any contemporary examples of things that have started small and then grown over time (companies, churches, teams, etc.)? What, if anything, do they have in common?

3. When discouraged by small beginnings or a lack of immediate success, where do you find encouragement?

4. How would you explain to someone else the idea that, with God, little is big?

5. As you read the verses from Zechariah, what encouragements or challenges do they bring to you?

6. What current project are you working on for God that you should recommit to him in prayer and practice?

7. In practical terms, how can you place your faith in God's care for your future and find hope in his plans for you today?

Jesus answered and said to her, "Whoever drinks of this water will thirst again, but whoever drinks of the water that I shall give him will never thirst. But the water that I shall give him will become in him a fountain of water springing up into everlasting life."

—John 4:13–14 NKJV

9

A Church for the Thirsty

During the time period when I had been praying, commuting, and beginning to plant Overflow Church, I was also getting to know people in our new communities of Benton Harbor and St. Joseph. In many ways I didn't fit in to either of our communities. I typically wore jeans and sandals, and I drove an older economy car. Then in my late twenties, my hair often needed a bit of help (spiked and messy), and I had far more passion than experience. During this season, I wrestled to the ground two important things in my life and in the vision for Overflow Church. The first was that if God called me to Benton Harbor and St. Joseph, he surely knew what he was doing and what he was getting.

So even though I felt out of place at times, I decided I would be myself and not try fit the mold of others. I would respectfully establish my own identity even dress code. (I wear jeans to this day, often with a sport coat, and the sandals are always close by.)

Second, while I was studying the Bible and journaling on the beaches of Lake Michigan (definitely a perk of our new community), I discovered that God was specifically calling Overflow Church to be a church for the thirsty. As I read Jesus' interaction with the Samaritan woman at the well in John 4, I saw that many in our community shared her thirst. It's a thirst deep within the human soul, a fundamental longing placed within us by our Creator. It is a thirst that only Jesus can satisfy through a relationship with him.

Jesus did the unthinkable to reveal himself to the Samaritan woman as living water. Setting aside any concern about the opinions of others, Jesus crossed racial, gender, and social boundaries to share a conversation, a cup of water, love, and truth with this woman. I felt certain this is exactly what he would do through Overflow Church. It would be a gathering place for the thirsty, a place where the unchurched and de-churched (those who left the church or were wounded by it) could come to experience Jesus free from the hurts and hang-ups often associated with church and with religion itself. We would be a church that flowed over the boundaries of race, class, and even church backgrounds. We would be an overflow church.

We soon had the privilege of seeing this vision unfold. A woman began to come to our storefront office on her lunch breaks to talk about life and faith. Although she made it clear that she hated the church and believed there were many pathways to God, she slowly began to embrace Jesus. Before long, she and some from her household decided to follow Jesus and were baptized. She was thirsty, and we had the honor of creating a modern-day well, a place where she could enter into a life-changing relationship with Jesus.

Jesus demonstrated amazing compassion for people regardless of their backgrounds. As water flows from the highest point to the lowest, he moved from the highest point in heaven to the lowest places on earth to meet people wherever they were. In John 4, we see that Jesus chose not to avoid Samaria, the despised region of the day, but traveled right through the heart of it. He demonstrated his humanity by asking for a drink, and his divinity by revealing himself as the giver of living water. Jesus met this woman right where she was in her time of need, and he was humble enough to ask for her help as well. I believe our exchanges with people should always be a two-way street marked by humility, love, and an openness to receive help from them as well as give it. If we are to live like Jesus, we too will overflow to those around us. As Bible scholar F. F. Bruce stated, "The living water which the woman received from Jesus had certainly become an overflowing fountain in her life, and others were coming to share the refreshment that she had begun to enjoy. Let us not grow weary in well-doing; the most unlikely soul may prove the most effective witness."[1]

Maybe you have given up on yourself, on someone you care about, or on "those people" in our world. May Jesus' ministry to the Samaritan woman give you hope that he does have the ability to transform any life, and to realize that it is often the most unlikely people who are used by God.

Discussion Questions and Application

At Overflow Church, we identify nine actions we believe a "church for the thirsty" will commit to and live out. The discussion questions for this chapter are embedded in this list of actions.

1. Be a community of people hungering and thirsting for more of God in our daily lives (see Ps. 42:1–2; Matt. 5:6). Do you hunger and thirst for more of God? Explain.

2. Embrace all people regardless of race, economic status, social status, and background (see John 4:1–10). What comes

to mind when you think of embracing all people regardless of their background? What excites, challenges, and scares you about this?

3. Meet people where they are in life, taking the message of Christ's love and goodness to the streets (see John 4:11–13). In what ways have you seen the message of Christ's love taken "to the streets" and beyond the walls of a church?

4. Help people see that Jesus is the true source of life both now and eternally (see John 4:13–14). If you were speaking with an unchurched person, how would you explain that Jesus is the true source of life?

5. Extend grace and mercy to people regardless of their lifestyles (see John 4:15–18). What challenges have you experienced in being gracious with people who have sinful lifestyles?

6. Speak the truth in love and challenge people to move forward with Christ and to leave their sins behind (see John 4:18). In what specific ways can we lovingly challenge people to move forward by applying the truth of the Bible to their lives?

7. Celebrate God and life through a true spirit of worship that is focused on worshiping from the heart regardless of worship style or location (see John 4:21–24). What challenges have you experienced in moving beyond familiar

worship styles and locations to truly worship God in spirit and truth? How have you dealt with those challenges?

8. Be patient with others and ourselves as we all discover what it means to follow Jesus (see John 4:25–26). In what areas do you need to develop patience with yourself and others as you "learn to passionately follow Jesus?

9. Mobilize people to live out the mission and share the good news with their friends, families, coworkers, and communities (see John 4:27–30, 39–42). With whom could you share the good news of Jesus this week? In what ways could you mobilize others to spread his love and hope?

Note

1. F. F. Bruce, *The Gospel of John* (Grand Rapids, MI: Eerdmans, 1983), 115.

Then I said to them, "You see the distress that we *are* in, how Jerusalem *lies* waste, and its gates are burned with fire. Come and let us build the wall of Jerusalem, that we may no longer be a reproach." And I told them of the hand of my God which had been good upon me, and also of the king's words that he had spoken to me. So they said, "Let us rise up and build." Then they set their hands to *this* good *work*.

—Nehemiah 2:17–18 NKJV (emphasis added)

10

Launching a Shared Vision

For a vision to become reality, it must engage and empower others to participate in fulfilling it. A great vision is a shared vision, and sharing a vision requires relationships. During the early days of Overflow Church, we carried the vision wherever we went and invited others to be a part of it. Whether we were in the mall office, doing outreach in the community, or holding Bible studies, we shared the vision and asked others to join us. In the late fall of 2007, we decided to take this a step further by holding vision parties at a local coffee shop in the newly created arts district of Benton Harbor. Our goal was to gather forty people at each party and share the vision, answer questions, and invite people to join us in launching Overflow Church in early 2008. Each party included music, dessert, a short vision talk, and a time for questions and discussion.

By God's grace, those vision parties produced exactly what we had hoped for. Roughly forty people from those vision parties joined our launch team. As we then met with them, the questions they asked were always refreshing and their input was helpful in refining our vision. Dr. Bob Lupton, an author and community development leader in Atlanta for the past forty years, compares shared vision to an uninflated balloon that has an unknown shape.[1] As each person breathes life into the balloon (or vision), its shape is revealed. By the time it is completed, the balloon (or vision) has a different shape and form than initially expected, but each person feels a sense of ownership because it was created together.

Through our early vision parties and launch team meetings, the vision for Overflow Church truly became a shared vision. The forty people who joined our launch team spent a great deal of time together planning, praying, and preparing for the public launch of Overflow a few months later. One particular moment perfectly illustrates this vision sharing. Someone had asked why we couldn't give our service an odd start time that would be memorable and communicate that we were fun and different from other churches. So together we decided that our start time would be 10:31 a.m., using this as a marketing tactic. By combining our gifts and talents as a team, and saturating all we did in prayer, God produced a launch service that hosted 141 people! A shared vision multiplies, and that is what happened at Overflow Church.

Overflow Church began with small Bible studies, outreach at a housing project, and meeting people right where they were in life, particularly through our mall office. Throughout the early months, we continually shared the vision that God had given us and watched it become a vision that was shared by others. When a vision is God's, it naturally invites others to participate, which empowers them to have a voice in and ownership of the vision.

Nehemiah's story gives us a beautiful picture of how to launch a shared vision. Nehemiah was first given a burden, born of the distress and ruin of the city of Jerusalem. He took that burden to the Lord in prayer and fasting, which gave birth to a vision. Wisely, Nehemiah waited for the right time, then boldly shared his vision with the king, who responded favorably. Nehemiah then moved to share this vision with others. It is important to note, however, that Nehemiah didn't rush to share the vision with others too quickly. He first took the time to survey the land, praying and preparing for the moment when he would invite others to join the vision. When that moment came, Nehemiah was prepared and the shared vision was launched (see Neh. 2:17–18).

Has God given you a vision that has become dead or dormant? Perhaps this vision must be bathed in prayer, shared with others, and launched as a shared vision. We see in Nehemiah that everyone worked together and rebuilt the city walls in just fifty-two days. Maybe you need to spend more time with God and sharing your vision with others before giving up on it. Launching a shared vision is an exercise in prayer, patience, and relationship building, and it is one of the most exciting things you can do. We held our first public service for Overflow Church on March 16, 2008, as a shared vision — shared with God and with those he had brought to us. In the days since, many more people have come to believe in Christ and share in this great work. It is time for you to take your burden to God in prayer and let that give birth to his vision. May that vision be launched as you share it with others and ecourage them to join you.

Discussion Questions

1. Have you ever been part of starting something new or known someone who has? What was that process like?

2. Has God given you a vision for your life and ministry? How did this vision get started in your life?

3. When you consider how a burden bathed in prayer gives birth to a vision, what thoughts come to mind? Explain.

4. How would you describe the difference between a human-centered vision and a God-centered vision?

5. How would you describe the difference between launching a vision versus launching a shared vision based on the examples of Nehemiah and Overflow Church?

6. It took only fifty-two days for Nehemiah's vision to become reality. It has taken far longer than that for Overflow Church. How do those two examples inform your current situation?

7. What is your next step in either developing a God-given vision or sharing that vision with others?

Note

1. "Bob Lupton on Shared Vision," Vimeo video, posed by "DVULI," accessed September 17, 2015, https://vimeo.com/7187197.

PART 3

Love's Goal

So I sent messengers to them, saying, "I am doing a great work, so that I cannot come down. Why should the work cease while I leave it and go down to you?" But they sent me this message four times, and I answered them in the same manner.

—Nehemiah 6:3–4 NKJV

11

Loving Your Supporters and Your Critics

Anytime we do something we view as significant for God, our hopes are high and we want everyone to feel the same way. However, I have learned from painful experience that not everyone will share our dreams. It was just a few days prior to the launch of Overflow Church. We had cast our vision and gathered people to help us launch the church, and we were making new friendships that would be forged into a new family. As our launch team continued to grow, so did our love for our new friends and extended family called Overflow Church.

Cindy and I had read in a number of books on church planting that, although you want everyone to stay with you forever, some people will abandon the work in its early stages. These folk become "scaffolding," meaning that they come for a short season to help get the church going and prop it up, then drop away just as things are taking shape. Though we had been told about this phenomenon, we were naïve enough to think it would never happen to us. And we certainly never thought people might try to sabotage what we were doing. It is easy to love those who love you, but love is tested when we have to love those who are not the supporters, friends, or family you thought they were.

One day just prior to the launch of our first worship celebration, a family from the launch team asked to meet with me for coffee. I had hoped their intent was to share their enthusiasm and ideas concerning the launch, but it turned out to be quite the opposite. Their agenda centered on criticism of my leadership and, in particular, the absence of a proven model for the kind of church we were planting. The temperature in the room rose quickly as I feared this last-minute conference to be a potential threat to the success of the launch. Thankfully, though the temperature rose among us, our love for each other did as well. This was not the kind of unified love I had expected among the team members but the respectful, agree-to-disagree love that sees people of a different mind-set as brothers and sisters nonetheless. It was a love that maintained our broader connection in the kingdom of

God while agreeing to part ways on the launch of Overflow Church. Because of that love, we continue to count this family as friends in our community to this day.

Love's goal is something bigger than creating friends and proponents. It is treating others as brothers and sisters in Christ as we put the work of ministry ahead of personal viewpoints or agendas. Thankfully, Overflow found some new team members just a few days later who were able to fill in what we needed. God knew our need all along, and he brought them right to us.

Nehemiah, as the visionary behind rebuilding Jerusalem's walls, experienced the power of both encouragement and criticism. Just as church leaders do today, Nehemiah encountered those who were excited about what he was doing and those who were instantly critical. In Nehemiah 2:18–19, we see how quickly this tapestry of celebration and criticism unfolded: "And I told them of the hand of my God which had been good upon me, and also of the king's words that he had spoken to me. So they said, 'Let us rise up and build.' Then they set their hands to this good work. But when Sanballat the Horonite, Tobiah the Ammonite official, and Geshem the Arab heard of it, they laughed at us and despised us, and said, 'What is this thing that you are doing? Will you rebel against the king?" (NKJV). What a roller coaster of emotion this must have been for Nehemiah!

As you consider your life, you will undoubtedly discover there are supporters of you and the work you are doing. That is encouraging. You will also find critics, some who would like nothing better than to see you fail in the work God has called you to. That will be painful indeed. As the story of Overflow Church has unfolded, I've seen that some folks believed in the work almost immediately and had joined us to champion it. At the same time, there were a few lurkers among us, silent critics who eventually revealed themselves and tried to act as negative influences on the work through distraction and discouragement. Whenever we encountered such critics, our leadership team considered this central question: "Is what they're saying true, and, if so, how should it change our course as a result?" When we found criticism to be valid, we changed accordingly. When we did not, we ignored it and kept working. As Nehemiah said, "I am doing a great work, so that I cannot come down. Why should the work cease while I leave it and go down to you?" (Neh. 6:3 NKJV).

You must be able to stay the course in the face of criticism when you are certain you are on the course God has given you. Both supporters and critics come with any work from God. Don't put too much weight on what either say. Instead, let your supporters encourage you, and turn your critics into coaches by considering whether what they say is true and how it can help you grow.

Discussion Questions

1. Supporters and critics seem to be everywhere via social media and in person. When difficult or negative feedback is received, how can you tell the difference between criticism that comes from a supportive heart and that which comes from a critical spirit?

2. How have you handled criticism in the past? Do you put too much, just enough, or not enough weight on it?

3. In what specific ways can you learn from critics and allow them to become your coaches?

4. What does Nehemiah's response to those who directly opposed and even tried to sabotage his work teach you about responding to opposition (see Neh. 6:3)?

5. Have you ever let a supporter or critic have too much control over you? Describe how that happened and the result. What did you learn through that experience that you can apply in the future?

The Word became flesh and blood, and moved into the neighborhood.
—John 1:14 MSG

12

Welcome to the Neighborhood

Jesus summed up all of the law in two commandments: Love God and love your neighbor (see Matt. 22:37–38). This teaching is central to our calling as believers, and we spend a good deal of time considering how to love our neighbors. It is interesting, though, that we ignore this command when selecting the neighborhoods in which we live. Some of us live only where we are able, and others live wherever we want. For the latter, safety, schools, and the resale value of homes tend to be important factors in choosing a neighborhood. Jesus, however, had no such concerns. In *The Message*, Eugene Peterson said that Jesus "moved into the neighborhood" (John 1:14 MSG). He came and dwelt among us here on earth. The incarnation was the ultimate act of neighboring. Jesus gave up the very best neighborhood— heaven—to live on our block.

When we moved to the Benton Harbor and St. Joseph area, we first lived in a small apartment in a neighboring community. This choice was driven by economic necessity, and the experience proved humbling. We could not afford much, and our family of four lived in a tiny, 700-square-foot apartment with no laundry, dishwasher, or microwave; holes in the bathroom floorboards; and a furnace that failed six times that winter. (The apartment complex has since been condemned and torn down.) During that six-month period, God clarified our calling to love our neighbors and to live within the Benton Harbor community. We soon moved into a modest rental house in Benton Harbor and felt as if we had moved into a mansion.

In this new house we began to learn what it means to love our neighbors. As the only white family in the neighborhood at the time, with the majority of the neighborhood being made up of blacks, we were met with mixed reactions. One day we came home to find a dead raccoon placed in our driveway as a welcoming gift. We received stares of suspicion. And then God began to move. We prayed that the drug dealers working in our alley would move down the road, and they did. We helped pick up trash, shared popsicles and yard toys with the children in our neighborhood, helped with basic home repairs and painting, mowed lawns, and did our best to show love and kindness to those living around us.

Over time, one act of love and kindness led to another, and today many of our core families and a few of our key leaders live in that same neighborhood as relationships developed and they chose to become a part of Overflow Church. That didn't happen overnight, and God had to bring us through a number of difficult experiences. But when we see our homes less as real estate and more as relationship builders, Jesus can really begin to work.

God spoke a beautiful word through Jeremiah to those in Babylonian captivity. He told them to "build houses and settle down; plant gardens and eat what they produce. Marry and have sons and daughters; find wives for your sons and give your daughters in marriage, so that they too may have sons and daughters. Increase in number there; do not decrease" (Jer. 29:5–6). Can you imagine? They were in a place they did not choose, under the control of people who had mistreated them, and in a culture they did not yet understand. Despite that, God asked them to engage in the life of that community and be good neighbors (see v. 7). Throughout Scripture, God demonstrated his desire to dwell with and among his people. He is intensely relational and wants his people to have that same passion for community. Live with and for God and those in your neighborhood. As Cindy and I chose a home for ourselves, we found ourselves in a neighborhood that we would fall in love with and where we would see great fruit. Yet it took faith to see what God saw in that place.

When you look at your neighborhood and your neighbors, what do you see? Do you see opportunities to make friends, show Christ's love, and make a difference? Or do you see obstacles with names? Be honest with yourself, then begin to see the power of Jesus' life and example in the midst of your current neighborhood. "The Word became flesh and blood, and moved into the neighborhood" (John 1:14 MSG). Jesus was born into this world because of God's great love for us (see John 3:16). That's why he moved into our neighborhood. In your neighborhood, or as you consider your next move, how could you follow Jesus' example? If your neighbors were polled today, would they say you are an incarnation of love or that something changed for the better when you moved in?

Do not feel weighed down or discouraged; instead, be inspired by thinking about what your next steps with Jesus might lead to in your neighborhood. Look around you and let any "obstacle with a name" become an opportunity to be Jesus in the neighborhood. Over the past few decades, there has been a shift from the front porch to the back deck as the place where families spend time at home. Add to this the popularity of privacy fences and indoor entertainments, and you will realize the challenge of getting to know your neighbors in our culture. Maybe it's time to look over the fence or sit on the front porch in order to see what Jesus sees in your neighborhood.

Discussion Questions

1. How long have you lived in your neighborhood, and how did you end up there?

2. Do you see your neighbors more as obstacles with names or as opportunities? Explain.

3. How many of your neighbors do you know today? What might you do to know your neighbors better?

4. What factors make it difficult to get to know your neighbors? What might you do to overcome those challenges?

5. In what ways might you "look over the fence" or "move to the front porch" in order to see what Jesus sees in your neighborhood?

6. What other practical steps could you take in the coming weeks to live, love, and be like Jesus in your neighborhood?

For we are His workmanship, created in Christ Jesus for good works, which God prepared beforehand that we should walk in them.

—Ephesians 2:10 NKJV

13

Prepared in Advance

After we moved to Benton Harbor and the ministry began picking up steam, it became clear that God had prepared this Christ-centered movement in advance. One of my favorite verses, then and now, is Ephesians 2:10: "For we are His workmanship, created in Christ Jesus for good works, which God prepared beforehand that we should walk in them" (NKJV). Time after time in the early days of Overflow, and still today, we would walk into a situation that we just knew God had prepared for us long before we were even aware of it.

One such occasion concerned our need for a bus to transport people in our community to church and other events. With almost nothing in the bank account and our offerings quite meager, I had dismissed the idea of acquiring a bus. However, within a few months of our public launch, a gentleman in the church asked me if we wanted a bus. I said yes but quickly added that we had no money for one. He asked me to join him at an auction the following week where, true to his word, he bought and donated our first fifteen-passenger van. As if that was not enough to prove that God had prepared this good work in advance, within the next thirty days another gentleman volunteered as a bus driver and a third donated a premier paint job from one of the top companies in Chicago. God had orchestrated not only the vehicle itself but also the resources required to take this outreach ministry to another level.

Over the years, God has reminded us that this ministry has been and always will be his. We have had many interesting experiences with that van, from using it as a moving truck to having the doors literally fall off while transporting a vanload of high school football players to church. In each case, God provided what we needed to keep moving forward. Just recently we received word that another volunteer has committed to being a driver in this ministry and another donor has pledged to provide vans next year. God has prepared his work in advance, and we are blessed to watch his plan unfold.

The old saying holds that "where God guides, he provides." Have you ever faced a task you were not sure you could complete or possibly didn't know what it would take to complete it? Overflow's story is like that. We have watched God reveal his plan one step at a time, then reveal his provision as well. God is at work. We simply need to trust the provision he has already made.

Taking a closer look at Ephesians 2:10, we learn four important truths, all made possible because of our relationship with Christ: (1) God sees us as his workmanship, or masterpiece; (2) we were created for good works—for a purpose; (3) God has prepared everything about this good work in advance; and (4) we simply need to walk forward, trusting God to provide. This is so encouraging! If you were to picture a potter shaping a piece of pottery, a sculptor chiseling a sculpture, or a painter painting on his or her canvas, this is what God is doing in each of our lives as he shapes, molds, and fashions us into his image. As God shapes you in and for his purpose, he is simply bringing out the masterpiece in you. That is, "Christ in you, the hope of glory" (Col. 1:27 NKJV).

To walk forward believing God has already prepared for our work requires faith—this is different from moving recklessly, based on our own vision or desire. God doesn't want us to run ahead of him but to walk faithfully with him.

At Overflow we discovered God knew we needed a bus ministry even before we did, and he showed us how he had prepared for it. He will do the same for you.

Discussion Questions

1. How does Overflow's story with the bus ministry speak to you? Explain.

2. When and how have you seen God's provision in your own life?

3. What comes to mind when you consider that in Christ you are God's workmanship, masterpiece, or work of art?

4. In what ways does the fact that you are being shaped and molded by God challenge or encourage you today?

5. When you consider that God has a purpose for you and has already prepared what you need to fulfill it, how does that change your view of your work?

6. Are you running, walking, or sitting still with what God has given you to do? How do you understand the difference between those three options?

7. What steps could you take today to move forward with Christ and his plans for your life?

Then He said, "What is the kingdom of God like? And to what shall I compare it? It is like a mustard seed, which a man took and put in his garden; and it grew and became a large tree, and the birds of the air nested in its branches."

—Luke 13:18–19 NKJV

14

What Is Kingdom Success?

Overflow Church got off to a great start with 141 people in attendance on the first day. However, no one prepared me for what would happen the following week and every week thereafter for several months. Our attendance dropped to 106, then stayed under one hundred for seven months. A few years earlier, I had my first experience preaching at a weekend service. It was in front of more than two thousand people. Now God was asking me to serve him with only a fraction of that number in attendance. To say God was humbling me would be an understatement. However, to say God was helping me redefine success according to kingdom values would be very accurate.

I battled discouragement through that process and began to question what we were doing. I found myself doubting whether God was still with us and even wondered if we had made a mistake in starting Overflow Church. Things went from bad to worse when I started comparing our story to the perceived success of others. The comparison game always leads to a downward spiral, and I was circling toward the bottom quickly. Overflow looked more and more like a failure to me each week. The problem was my expectations. My version of success had nothing to do with the kingdom of God and its measures of accomplishment.

Slowly but surely God began to lift my eyes to see what he was doing through Overflow Church. Though worship service attendance numbers disappointed me, God began to show how he was drawing people to himself through the week in outreach and discipleship ministries. The church was developing a solid core and creating an atmosphere of love and hospitality. On Sundays, rather than seeing the empty seats at our worship services, I began to see the seats that were already filled with people being transformed by God's love. God worked on my heart during those months to reconfigure my vision of success. As my personal calling continued to take shape, it was clear that God had called us to this community to start not only a church but also a nonprofit Christian community development center. As I became acquainted with other leaders from churches, businesses, government, and nonprofits, God helped me see that his kingdom is far bigger and broader than Overflow Church.

As my metrics became aligned with God's kingdom and what he was already doing in the Benton Harbor and St. Joseph communities, I had a greater sense of contentment. My focus would be on the quality of the work God had given us to do, not just the quantity. During this season, I noticed that many of the people we reached in the community would rediscover a walk with Jesus through Overflow's ministry then become involved in another church. Frustrating as that was, and still can be, it is a win for the kingdom to see people come back to Jesus and his church. God was showing me that we were to be a kingdom vehicle that measured success according to his values, which meant we were not in control of the results, neither could we always measure them. To live in the tension between what you see happening—that is, what you can measure—and what you believe is happening below the surface is the definition of trust! My ability to trust God has grown tremendously over the years as a result of those early lessons at Overflow. I have embraced his kingdom metrics, which are centered on being faithful and obedient stewards of what God has called us to.

Our society's definition of success has greatly influenced Christian culture and the church. In Western Christianity, our vision of success is often patterned after large ministries and the numbers they generate. We measure the things we can readily see. Though God certainly does produce fruitfulness, often on a large scale, holding that as our vision for success owes more to the world's standards than to the kingdom's. We must step back and consider that bigger, better, and more are not necessarily in God's plan for each situation, and his plan definitely does not run on our timetable.

I was in my midtwenties when I preached my first sermon to an audience of over two thousand people. That early "success" meant the move to Overflow Church required a radical adjustment in my thinking. I discovered that God's kingdom metrics were very different from my own. I learned kingdom success is based on faithfulness and obedience and results in a steady, growing influence that often operates below the surface and is therefore not measurable. In Luke 13:18–19, we learn that the kingdom of God is like a mustard seed, which starts extremely small. We know that these plants develop an extensive root system beneath the surface long before they become visible above ground. By the time the plant appears, it is deeply rooted and ready for visible growth—just like the church.

Are you discouraged because you have measured your success based on comparisons with the world and its timing? Let God adjust your metrics to reflect kingdom values, and experience a new freedom to faithfully and obediently follow him.

Discussion Questions

1. How do you measure success in your life? What measurements do you use to set your goals and evaluate progress?

2. What is the difference between the world's definition of success and kingdom metrics? List examples that come to mind.

3. Have you been in a situation where you realized that God's results were going to look different from what you anticipated? How did you feel? How did you respond?

4. What are some ways we can deal with the space between our expectations and God's purposes?

5. Read Philippians 4:1–13. How do the ideas of contentment and relying on Christ's strength enable you to wait on God's plan?

6. Read Luke 4:16–21. What are some of the kingdom values that Christ held, and in what ways might they influence our view of success?

And when Jesus came to the place, He looked up and saw him, and said to him, "Zacchaeus, make haste and come down, for today I must stay at your house." So he made haste and came down, and received Him joyfully. But when they saw it, they all complained, saying, "He has gone to be a guest with a man who is a sinner."

—Luke 19:5–7 NKJV

15

Real Life, Real People, Real God

As stated earlier, the mission of Overflow Church is to reach the unchurched and de-churched in our world, journeying together as we learn how to passionately follow Jesus and joyfully serve others. It is a mission centered on the life, ministry, and message of Jesus Christ. We desire to meet people right where they are in life, just as Jesus did. As I researched our county's demographics, I learned that more than half of the population had no religious affiliation. I also consistently met people who had attended a church at one time but had left organized religion due to hurts or hang-ups. As I met with these people in our mall office, in public places, and in local businesses, I realized that they were incredibly open to talking about their faith. As I asked questions and listened intently, I experienced the power of being real with people. Jesus engaged real people in a way that transformed their lives and our world. I tried to follow his example. Through these conversations, I began to see our very real God move in real life with real people.

I remember one young mother who frantically rushed into our mall office just as I was closing for the day. She swept in with three small children in tow and asked if we had a bathroom. We did, which was fortunate because one of her children had an emergency in progress. After the disaster was avoided, I asked how she was doing. It was a simple question, asked casually but sincerely. She burst into tears and began to relate how difficult her life was. That impromptu conversation led to ongoing talks with others in our church, eventually resulting in her conversion to Christ and baptism. Frankly, her walk with the Lord and relationship with Overflow Church is shaky to this day. Real life is messy. But our God is real, and his love makes our messes into something beautiful. That transformation began for this woman with the very real need of having to find a bathroom. I'm so glad we were there for her and her children.

Around that same time, I was preaching on Ezekiel 47 and Overflow Church was discussing what it means to put our toes in the water of faith. This young woman described her new faith as putting her toes in the water. This powerful metaphor symbolizes stepping into the life that flows from God, then going deeper and deeper into it. As the river flows and we step in deeper, our lives flourish. Ezekiel 47:12 says, "Fruit trees of all kinds will grow on both banks of the river. Their leaves will not wither, nor will their fruit fail. Every month they will bear fruit, because the water from the sanctuary flows to them. Their fruit will serve for food and their leaves for healing." As God flows in our community, we see lives flourishing and healing taking place among very real people. The communities we serve have been physically separated by the St. Joseph River, yet God's river of life overflows on both sides with hope and healing in very real ways.

As you move through an ordinary day, the things you notice and the people with whom you interact can have a much greater effect on your life than you may realize. Our ability to be aware of and interact with the world God has placed us in may be one of the least explored areas of our faith. Throughout Scripture we see that God is continually at work in his world, engaging his people and expanding both their horizons and the reach of his kingdom. It would be interesting to learn how much we miss each day because we're simply not paying attention. The late Dallas Willard said, "The overarching biblical command is to love, and the first act of love is always the giving of attention."[1] When Jesus met Zacchaeus, the simple act of giving attention to a very real person led to God's love being shown in a real-life situation. The same could be said of the woman in the mall office. Giving attention to real people leads to real-life encounters with God.

To whom could you pay more attention and perhaps see God at work as a result? You could be on the verge of a tremendous breakthrough with God as you get in touch and in step with what is happening around you. Real-life situations often emerge at the strangest times and places, yet they can lead to the greatest real-life changes.

We have been talking about the real lives of other people, but what about your own? God loves you in a real way just as you are. What would change in your life if you fully embraced the truth that God loves you and wants to be a part of your life in a real way? Our lives are transformed as our faith in God moves from religion to relationship. May your life be transformed as well, and may you move from putting your toes in the water to diving into this new life and letting God have his way.

Discussion Questions

1. Reflect on what God is doing in your life, what he is doing around you, and what he is doing in the people he has placed in your path. What do you notice and how does that challenge or encourage you?

2. How could the idea of paying attention to life, people, and situations change your approach to daily living?

3. What is the difference between a religion and a relationship with God? Which would you say better characterizes your faith? Why?

4. What does it mean to move from putting your toes in the water with God to diving into the deep end? How might you do this?

5. What comes to your mind when you hear that God is real, loves real people, and engages in real life?

6. What are some things you could do to better pay attention to those around you and help them experience God?

Note

1. Dallas Willard, *The Spirit of the Disciplines: Understanding How God Changes Lives* (San Francisco: HarperCollins 1988), 210.

PART 4

Doing a New Thing

The one who plants and the one who waters have one purpose, and they will each be rewarded according to their own labor. For we are co-workers in God's service; you are God's field, God's building.

—1 Corinthians 3:8–9

16

Planting, Watering, and Loving

Any new initiative brings a sense of excitement and wonder. It causes us to dream of what could be. When that dream begins to include others, it really gets exciting. As Overflow Church came into being, we were joined by new friends who dreamed with us. It was an exciting time as God brought the right people at the right time every step of the way. When a bus driver, a media director, a website developer, or a financial consultant was needed, God provided the perfect person in each case. In those early days, we often referred to Jim Collins's metaphor from the book *Good to Great*, in which he describes an organization as a bus.[1] First, you need to get the right people on the "bus," then figure out where to drive it. God was putting the right people on the bus at the right time. We also found that seats on the bus would change for some or be moved around. For some the bus ride itself was a temporary season.

In 1 Corinthians 3:6–8, the apostle Paul said, "I planted, Apollos watered, but God gave the increase. So then neither he who plants is anything, nor he who waters, but God who gives the increase. Now he who plants and he who waters are one, and each one will receive his own reward according to his own labor" (NKJV). These verses are a great reminder that God has a plan and purpose for the people involved in the church in each season of its life. The key is to trust the process and love each person through that season. That isn't always easy. At Overflow, what began with excitement and wonder led to frequent disappointments as friends moved on and some relationships ended. The revolving door began to turn in years two through five, and we were not prepared for the emotional toll. As people came and went, fulfilling their role and season at Overflow, we celebrated their contributions but grieved their loss. In time we saw that God always had someone else on the way to help with the next stage of his plan. God is truly faithful, and we have learned to trust him with the seasons and keep love at the center of our lives and ministry. When God's love permeates our relationships with people, the roles they play are blessed and his work advances. It is difficult to love people fully and intentionally yet be willing to let them move on, but that is the exact role of a shepherd in God's flock.

God works through people, but his ultimate work unfolds not through one individual but through many generations (see Heb. 11). His purposes supersede our plans and ideas. His kingdom is for *his* glory, not ours. Each of us has a part to play in God's work, but none of us is irreplaceable. In ministry it is vital to get the right leaders on board but also to be flexible, as there will be transitions along the way.

In our enthusiasm to begin Overflow Church, this was something we overlooked. We naïvely believed everyone would be as passionate and committed to the work as we were and would remain for the long term. We were unprepared for the emotional and practical toll that leadership transitions would take. During some seasons, leaders were coming, going, and switching roles for reasons we didn't fully understand or agree with, leading to some difficult moments that exposed areas in which I, and others, needed to grow. Yet through it all, we loved one another and were excited to watch things change before our eyes. Though these seasons were difficult for Cindy and me, God's grace was always present, and we have experienced healing and renewed hope as we comprehend God's larger purpose in those transitions.

Have you been through a season of transition with people recently? Have you considered that these transitions are vital for the work to grow, for you to grow, and for others to grow? The seasons change four times each year, and each one looks completely different from the last and plays its own vital role in the growth process. When you can see the transitions in your life in this way, you will find greater peace in your work. Whether you are planting, watering, or harvesting, be faithful to what God has for you in this season. Do not deviate from his plans. Rely on his strength, not your own. Trust him with the part you are to play, and know that God's plans and purposes always prevail.

Discussion Questions

1. How does the idea that God's purposes are far bigger than you yet include you personally impact you? Explain.

2. What season are you currently in: planting, watering, or harvesting? How can you stay faithful in this season?

3. Recall a time when someone on whom you depended moved to another season of life or ministry. What was it like?

4. Based on 1 Corinthians 3:8–9, how would you explain the significance of life-season transitions to someone who struggled to understand the concept?

5. What can you do to fully love and engage those around you even though you have previously been hurt or disappointed by changing seasons?

6. What would you say to encourage someone who is in a season of transition, or who is fulfilling the work they are supposed to be doing but feels discouraged? With whom should you share those words today?

7. How does the truth that God's plans and purposes always prevail encourage or challenge you in regard to your work?

Note

1. Jim Collins, *Good to Great: Why Some Companies Make the Leap . . . and Others Don't* (New York: Harper-Collins, 2001), 41.

17

A Backyard Full of Love

I was blessed to grow up in a neighborhood filled with children my age and with parents who invited neighborhood kids to bring their bikes and skateboards to play in our driveway. We didn't have an abundance of material things, but my parents did provide a sandbox, a fort, a few toys, and hearts full of love that welcomed my friends at any time. My mom and dad transformed our backyard into a safe haven for us. So when Cindy and I moved our family to Benton Harbor, we did the same in our new neighborhood. As we settled into our new home, Cindy boldly created an atmosphere of hospitality and love. She prayed over our home and neighborhood. She opened our window shades daily as a sign of hospitality. Friends began to give us children's toys for our small, fenced backyard. Our kids began to play there, and others soon joined them. Each day anywhere from six to twelve children could be found playing in "Miss Cindy's" backyard. People in the neighborhood began to wonder if we were running a day care!

God gave Cindy plenty of new ideas to reach those around us, and her small acts of hospitality and love began to grow. She offered snacks at our picnic table, along with a Bible story. Children gathered (ours included) to hear the stories and ask questions. As he heard the story of God our Creator, one child asked in amazement, "You mean I did not come from a genie in a bottle?" By simply loving our neighbors, welcoming children, and using what we had, we saw great breakthroughs. By our second year there, the group of a dozen or so children had grown to a backyard vacation Bible school for forty kids. By the third summer, Miss Cindy's backyard VBS included more than a hundred children and thirty adult volunteers, and it took up the entire block. We brought in a sound system, grilled hamburgers and hot dogs, and shared what we had with our neighbors. During this event, we were able to set up folding chairs in the middle of the street and talk with fifteen teenagers about life and faith.

Cindy also orchestrated a day of gardening to help neighbors plant flowers and landscape their yards. They were speechless, with tears in their eyes, looking at the beauty their hard work produced. They had never experienced that before.

During this time, Cindy also directed Splash, the children's ministry at Overflow Church. The ministry was growing fast, and when we needed a new children's ministry leader the baton was passed to a mother from our neighborhood whose children had attended the backyard Bible studies. Only God could orchestrate such an incredible sequence of events from a simple, yet profound, act of love. One act of intentional kindness led to another and another, and that cycle continues to this day.

When Jesus was asked what was the most important commandment, his simple summary no doubt astounded those listening (see Matt. 22:37–39). At the time of Jesus' ministry, the Pharisees had more than six hundred additional commands to God's law. By summing up all of this with such profound simplicity, Jesus clearly identified what it means to please God. We are to continually love God and love others. As we discovered with Overflow Church, that practical love of others can have an awesome impact on the world. When God's love grows within us, it inevitably flows through us to those around us. It will lead to using your home, backyard, driveway, vehicle, or whatever you have in ways you've never imagined. When God's love is at the center of who we are, everything you do will be shaped by that love—which results in loving your neighbors.

So who is your neighbor? It is anyone God places in your path. He wants to share his generous love with them through you. Have you considered how your neighbors need his love? What about your coworkers? God is love, and he will fill you with love so that it will overflow to those around you. Buckle up for the ride of your life, and ask God to help you share his love with your neighbors.

Discussion Questions

1. Would the people who know you well say that you truly love God and others? Explain your thoughts.

2. Who are your neighbors? Name some of those in your neighborhood, workplace, school, and community.

3. In what ways do your neighbors experience God's love through you?

4. On a scale of one to ten, how would you rate your current love for God? How would you rate your current love for your neighbors? Are you satisfied with the numbers you gave yourself? Why or why not?

5. What practical steps could you take this week to grow in your love for God?

6. We often grow in our love for our neighbors by getting to know and serving them. How could you do that this week?

As they traveled along the road, they came to some water and the eunuch said,
"Look, here is water. What can stand in the way of my being baptized?"
And he gave orders to stop the chariot. Then both Philip and the eunuch
went down into the water and Philip baptized him.

—Acts 8:36, 38

18

Celebrating Life with the Lord

Baptism is a celebratory sacrament of the church. It is a declaration of faith and a public witness of having been made new by Jesus Christ. It is an awesome, exuberant celebration that a friend of mine likens to spiking the football after a touchdown. Baptism is a highlight in the life of any congregation, and it is beautiful to be part of. Overflow conducted its first baptisms in a health club swimming pool in December 2007, and we have continued regularly ever since. We have been blessed to see more than two hundred people pass through the waters of baptism. We have celebrated their stories of coming to faith, and our faith has increased as well. In fact, as we conducted outdoor baptisms in Lake

Michigan, we faced a series of situations that God used to strengthen our faith as a church.

In the summer of 2008, we conducted our first lake baptisms. With a great sense of excitement, we left the movie theater where we held our morning worship service and headed for the lake. We looked forward to seeing our friends declare their faith and take this important step forward with Jesus. However, when we arrived at the beach, the height of the waves amazed us, and we wondered if we should proceed. Our excitement won out, and despite the dangerous conditions we ventured out to baptize people between the crashing waves. A few of the waves washed over my six-foot frame, but no harm came to any of us. As I look back on that day, I am filled with awe at God's hand upon us. He protected us beyond our understanding, and I'm sure he watched with joy as we celebrated new lives joining his kingdom.

In the summer of 2011, we decided to move our worship service to a pavilion at the lake in preparation for baptism. The thought was beautiful, but the weather was not. As we set up for the service, we kept any eye on the weather radar. A severe storm was on a straight path to our community. So we prayed for God to scatter the storm and send it around us so we could worship together and baptize in his beautiful creation. God answered in a powerful way as we watched the storm split into two parts and move around us to the north and south. We praised, worshiped, taught, and baptized twenty-six people that day. Everyone was awed by the hand of God, and our faith soared to new levels.

Though the weather had so far been iffy for outdoor baptisms, the next summer we again moved outside for our worship baptism service. Once again a summer storm was accelerating directly toward us. As we sang "Blessed Be Your Name," high wind and buckets of rain hit us and left us scrambling to disband our service. We delayed baptism for two more weeks due to riptides, then moved the service indoors. God didn't answer our prayers in the way we'd hoped, but he did teach us to sing "Blessed Be Your Name" with a full heart and celebrate life's changes regardless of how they take shape. We ended up doing the baptisms in a cattle trough in the empty Sears storefront that we had come to own. We still use that trough for baptisms at Overflow Church. It is a reminder that God provides, just not always in the ways we expect.

Overflow has been blessed to see the power of the gospel change lives. Baptism is the celebration of that life change. Commanded in Scripture (see Matt. 28:18–20) and modeled by Jesus (see Matt. 3:13–16), it is a powerful public witness to what Christ has done within the one who has repented and received Jesus as Lord. All baptisms are alike—yet different. Each person has his or her own unique story of encountering Jesus and believing in him for salvation. It is truly an incredible celebration, and it is meant for every believer in Christ. Have you celebrated your life with the Lord through baptism? If so, reflect on the experience and thank God for what he has done for you. If not, pray about taking that step in the near future.

Overflow has had many different experiences with baptism. We have baptized indoors and outdoors, in good weather and heavy storms, in a fitness club pool, at a borrowed church, in a lake, in a pond, and even in a cattle trough. Through all of these experiences, we have been reminded that the location and circumstances are unimportant. What matters is the celebration of what Jesus has done in someone's life and the step they take to publicly declare this through baptism. In Acts 8, we see that Philip experienced the power of God through his ministry. On a certain day and time, the Holy Spirit asked him to go immediately to a specific place by himself, far away from the action in the city. Philip responded with obedience, which led to an Ethiopian man finding new life through Jesus. New life with the Lord brings a new direction with new and unexpected outcomes. Jesus promised abundant life and joy, and that comes through saying "Yes!" to him.

Discussion Questions

1. If you have been baptized, what do you remember about the experience? Does it continue to have significance to you? How so?

2. If you have not been baptized as a believer, what is holding you back from taking that step?

3. How has your life changed since you became a follower of Jesus? What was your life like before Jesus? How did you come to Jesus? What has your life been like since receiving Jesus as Lord?

4. Imagine you are speaking with someone who has just been baptized as a believer. What advice or encouragement would you give about the new life that is ahead of him or her?

"But the time will come when the bridegroom will be taken from them; in those days they will fast." He told them this parable: "No one tears a piece out of a new garment to patch an old one. Otherwise, they will have torn the new garment, and the patch from the new will not match the old. And no one pours new wine into old wineskins. Otherwise, the new wine will burst the skins; the wine will run out and the wineskins will be ruined. No, new wine must be poured into new wineskins. And no one after drinking old wine wants the new, for they say, 'The old is better.'"

—Luke 5:35–39

19

New Wineskins

In 2005, while on staff at our previous church, I began to sense something missing in my life, leadership, and ministry. I could not put my finger on it but knew Jesus was calling me to something more. I reached out to a pastor in a neighboring community who had mentored me while I was in college and asked if he would be willing to meet. Over coffee we shared and caught up on all that had happened in the five years since we'd last met. I shared with him that I sensed something was missing and hoped he might have an answer. He wisely indicated that he wasn't sure but would be happy to meet for coffee each month so we could discuss the two things he was learning at the time. The first was a theology of the kingdom of God, and the second was the power of prayer and fasting. I was intrigued, and the journey began. During those meetings, God planted the seeds of what he would do in and through Overflow Church beginning in 2007.

In the early stages of planting Overflow, I began to realize how vital these conversations about the kingdom of God and about prayer and fasting would be for our new community. As I prayed, read, and researched potential church planting models that would fit our vision, I came up with nothing. I found bits and pieces of best practices, but never a resource that had the entire blend of church planting, Christian community development, and multi-cultural ministry that I believed God was calling us to. When reading Luke 5, I realized God had, in fact, given me a firm foundation for church planting with the practice of prayer and fasting because he was calling Overflow Church to be a new wineskin. New wineskins must stretch continually so God can pour into them what he wants to do next. Prayer and fasting, therefore, became a foundational practice and strategy in the work because it continually stretched us to accept more of what God had in mind.

Our first time of extended prayer and fasting as leaders of Overflow occurred in September 2008 during a sermon series called "Transformation." In 2010 our leadership started the New Year with a twenty-one-day period of prayer and fasting. In 2011 we invited the entire church to join us in a twenty-one-day fast, and we have continued this practice every New Year since. God has truly blessed these times of seeking him, and he has consistently given us the "new wine" we needed for the next season of ministry. During the fasting, he prepares us to receive. Overflow is a new wineskin today because we continue to pray, fast, and believe God always has new things to pour into it that will stretch us beyond ourselves. Personally, I believe the same has been true in my own life and leadership. God regularly stretches me in areas I rarely expect. The thing I realized was missing from my life in 2005 turned out to be this practice of prayer and fasting followed by an infusion of new wine. Overflow's leadership today participates in a weekly day of prayer and fasting, and we all find it to be a necessary part of keeping pace with God and his next steps for our journey.

Throughout Overflow's history, the practice of prayer and fasting has placed the church and its leadership in a better position to receive from God what he desires for the church and community. Over the years, we can attest to God moving significantly and specifically in two key areas in the church after the fast. The first key area is spiritual growth. The fast seems to set in motion a wave of spiritual growth in the church that includes new believers, new baptisms, and greater participation in weekly church attendance and activities. The second key area is leadership within the church. Many of our staff transitions and new hires have occurred in the six months immediately after the fast. Other individuals in the church have discovered the same unique movement and direction in their personal lives during the fast. They've been able to receive what God has next for them through this process in their marriage, family, work, or schooling.

If you're like I was before all this, you've probably heard others mention prayer and fasting but have not applied the practice yourself. Jesus was clear in Luke 5 that, while we wait on his return, we are to pray and fast in order to receive from him. Perhaps it is time for you to begin exploring the practice of prayer and fasting. Begin by studying God's Word on the subject, and reach out to others who have experience with it. The breakthrough in your walk with God and what he has next for your life may come as you seek him, undistracted, through prayer and fasting. This will help you receive his "new wine." Yes, your flesh will react against your spirit when it comes to fasting, but it will be well worth the effort. Try it, and see what God will do! May God pour into you all he has for you, and may you then overflow to the world around you!

Discussion Questions

1. What is your experience with the practice of prayer and fasting? What is the first thing that comes to mind when you hear these terms?

2. As you read Luke 5:35–39, what comes to mind when you think of new wine being poured into new wineskins? How do you think prayer and fasting might be part of the process of receiving new wine?

3. What stretches you in your view of God or the church?

4. Fasting can begin with skipping a meal or going without a food or additive (such as sugar or caffeine), or it can be for a full day or more. Where might God want you to start in the coming weeks and months? (Before beginning any dietary fast, it is recommended to first consult your physician.)

5. When we pray and fast, we set aside the things that we might run to in life when we're weary or confused in order to run to God instead. What are the things you turn to in time of need?

6. How might the practice of prayer and fasting help you replace those things you might run to with the presence of God himself?

7. What will you pray and fast over in the near future?

20

Stewardship of What God Gives

God has given us a tremendous responsibility here on earth. As we come into a relationship with Jesus, we begin to understand the deeper purposes and plans he has for our lives. He has given each of us resources—time, talent, and treasure—that take on new meaning in light of his plans for us. The issue in God's economy is not what we do or don't have. It's what we do with what he has given us. Author Ken Blanchard says that when we stand before God, the two most important questions will be, "What did you do with Jesus? [And] what did you do with the resources you were given in life?"[1] These two questions point to the importance of obedience and stewardship.

As the economy plunged in late 2008, Overflow faced its first significant leadership and stewardship challenges. As the economic crisis in America unfolded, we, like everyone else, faced a new reality. The income projected for our budget did not line up with expenses. I took a couple of months to watch, pray, and hope this reality would go away. It did not. As we approached the end of 2008, I realized it was time for action. I recall talking with a business leader I respected and lamenting the 40 percent budget cuts we were forced to make. As a new lead pastor, I was especially distraught at being forced to cut our meager staff salaries just before Christmas. As I bemoaned my situation, and the fact that these cuts would affect my own salary as well, this wise leader calmly helped me gain perspective. He said he too was facing cuts that year that would total ninety million dollars, and he was agonizing over it just as I was. I gasped and exclaimed that I really didn't have anything to complain about after listening to his story. Then he made a profound statement. He said, "I have learned over the years that whether the budget is big or small, the stress of making cuts is the same. In my case, there are just a few more zeroes attached to it." That statement helped me see that stewardship, whether in small things or larger ones, is still the same responsibility in God's eyes.

By God's grace, we did make our 40 percent budget cuts, and six months later we finished the year in the black with a small amount in savings to start our next ministry year. God graciously allowed our church to survive the downturn and positioned us for the future. Through that, we learned an invaluable lesson in stewardship. Throughout our brief history, we have often faced moments that required faith, action, generosity, and the ability to make the difficult decisions. We have learned to be good stewards. God has rewarded our stewardship over the years in awesome ways, and we have learned that great leadership requires facing difficult realities and making wise decisions with answers given by him.

Matthew 25:14–30 is a challenging passage for Christ followers. In this brief parable, Jesus made it clear that he gives each of us something we are not to sit on, but to steward for multiplication. It isn't enough to take what God has given us and just get by. Instead, we are to be good and faithful servants who make the most of what he gives us. Our faithfulness doesn't determine God's faithfulness. He is by nature faithful, with or without us. As we walk with him and carry out what he gives us to do, we're changed. This brings us to new levels of faith in him. The challenge of being a faithful steward is for every believer. It touches every area of life: home, work, church, and community.

Within this challenge is the mandate that we are not to make excuses or abdicate our responsibility to others. Whether the economy is good or bad, whether people support us or don't, and whether people understand us or don't, we are called to be faithful stewards. Our challenge is to trust God enough to faithfully walk through any circumstance side-by-side with him. Even when we have to make tough decisions and face brutal facts, God is faithful and will see us through. He has been there before us and walked through the same trials we face, and he knows the way.

Overflow faced tough moments that required faithful stewardship in difficult circumstances. You will face them too. As you do your part, trust that God will always do his. The results will be exactly what he desires. It is encouraging to recognize that God's desire is for the multiplication of his kingdom, and he will accomplish that through us as we are faithful stewards.

Discussion Questions

1. Read Matthew 25:14–30 in its entirety. What stands out to you about the idea of a "stewardship challenge"?

2. Which of the people in those verses most closely resembles you and your life? Explain.

3. What is your greatest challenge in being a faithful steward of what God has given you (your time, treasure, and talents)?

4. What steps do you need to take to become a faithful steward of what God has given you and to multiply it?

5. Are there any tough decisions and brutal facts you need to face? In what ways can you face them, not alone, but with others and in faith that God will help you through it?

Note

1. Ken Blanchard and Phil Hodges, *Lead Like Jesus: Lessons from the Greatest Leadership Role Model of All Time* (Nashville: W. Publishing Group, 2005), 112.

PART 5

Jars of Clay

"Have I not commanded you? Be strong and courageous. Do not be afraid; do not be discouraged, for the LORD your God will be with you wherever you go."

—Joshua 1:9

21

Charging the Darkness with a Flashlight

There are places in every community that people avoid. These are the places where "bad things" happen: a particular park or alleyway, a certain block, or an abandoned house down the street. We know darkness dwells there in a significant way, and we accept that. Starting in 2010, the pastor of a nearby African American congregation and I decided that we would not accept the darkness in Broadway Park in the city of Benton Harbor anymore. This park's reputation was notorious in our city. As we ate breakfast together one spring morning, we felt God leading us to do something about it. It was time for the church to join arms across denominational and racial lines and take the light into dark places. That breakfast meeting birthed a vision for an event at the park called H3: Hoops, Hip-Hop, and Hot Dogs. The event would be a show of unity and an opportunity to share the love of Christ through an innovative event. We had no funding, just a God-given burden that fueled a passionate love for our community. We knew our little would become much in God's hands. We felt that even if all we had was a "flashlight" of goodness, we would charge the darkness.

As we entered the park to see its condition, we were shocked by what we saw. It looked, as one local leader put it, like a jungle scene from the movie *Avatar*. We began to clean up and revitalize the park. During that first year, we experienced a true move of God as more than thirty volunteers from six churches joined hands to pray, pick up trash, and hold an awesome H3 event that served more than three hundred people. In 2011 the city of Benton Harbor expressed an interest in refurbishing a local park. We appealed to them on behalf of Broadway Park, which was not at all on their radar. Rather than refurbishing the park, the city decided to do a complete redevelopment of it. This was amazing to see as the place that was once avoided and feared became a beautiful and inviting space for everyone. Prior to the first H3 event (in 2010), we had filled hundreds of trash bags with litter and debris. Before the 2012 event, there were none—no trash bags were filled. God was on the move. At the 2013 H3 event, we rallied 175 volunteers from more than ten churches to serve over a thousand people. The joy, love, and unity of our community were evident throughout the day. The light of Christ had dispelled the darkness through his local body. It is incredible to witness what one spark of light can do. We impact our neighborhoods when we are willing to boldly love and live like Christ. Unified in him, we can change our cities for Christ and his kingdom.

As I reflect on what we observed at the H3 gathering on July 20, 2013, I continue to be amazed at Broadway Park's transformation, especially in light of what happened in that same neighborhood a decade earlier. In 2003 a high-speed chase, led primarily by white police officers, resulted in the death of a black male, who was riding a motorcycle in the neighborhood around Broadway Park. This death ignited what some referred to as a civil disturbance and others, including CNN, called a riot. Racial tensions that had been building for years in Benton Harbor erupted. What unfolded revealed how deep the racial and economic division between the communities really was. At that point, much work lay ahead to bring healing and transformation. Probably no one present at that time would have thought it possible. However, just ten years later, this same neighborhood was the scene of racial unity and healing. In Broadway Park, volunteers from all backgrounds and cultures came together to serve the neighborhood. New relationships were built between people. Healing began as people simply loved God and loved others. Even a little spark, a mere flashlight of love, pushes back the darkness. Light always conquers darkness. Darkness never overcomes light. And the brighter the light, the bigger the charge against darkness will be.

The Broadway Park transformation is what we might call the possible impossible. Two pastors lamenting the condition of a park in their community decided to do something about it. They put their faith into action. I wonder how many of these moments are missed, moments when we recognize a need, a challenge, a difficulty and think something should be done—yet we do nothing. Maybe you already have noticed a need for change in your community but wondered what could be done to help the situation. Let Overflow's story encourage you. These moments come from God. He knows that you can do all things through Christ who gives you strength (see Phil. 4:13). With him, all things are possible. He is the possible in impossible. As Joshua 1:9 says, "Have I not commanded you? Be strong and courageous. Do not be afraid; do not be discouraged, for the LORD your God will be with you wherever you go." Go with your God. Follow him! Your flashlight, whatever love you have, will break through the darkness in your community as he leads you.

Discussion Questions

1. What would your "Broadway Park" be?

2. What do you have in your hand today? What resources has God given you? What relationships and connections do you have that could help make a difference?

3. How does Joshua 1:9 speak to your situation? Where is God leading you today?

4. In what ways can you rest in the Joshua 1:9 promise as you follow God and move forward? Explain.

5. Are you ready to follow God wherever he may lead you? What excites you or challenges you about that possibility?

6. Great works for God are never done alone but rather in community, where the body of Christ is active, alive, and willing to give him all the glory. With whom do you need to share your burden for change? With whom might you partner on this incredible journey?

Now while Paul waited for them at Athens, his spirit was provoked within him when he saw that the city was given over to idols. Therefore he reasoned in the synagogue with the Jews and with the Gentile worshipers, and in the marketplace daily with those who happened to be there.

—Acts 17:16−17 NKJV

22

A Church without Walls

The idea that the church is a building is deeply embedded in our culture. We need a new understanding of what the church is meant to be—the *ecclesia* or "those called out" under the leadership of our head, Jesus. We speak of going to church and often compare churches based on the size and condition of the building and the number of people attending. However, the church is Jesus' bride, and it includes all of his followers in every nation throughout the world. When two or more gather in his name, he is present in their midst. As we started Overflow Church, we were intentional about finding gathering spaces in the marketplace, which led to renting space in a mall and a movie theater. We went where we could engage people as a "church without walls." In the beginning, that was easier because we didn't have a permanent facility. However, there was an ever-present pull toward establishing our own space. Somehow it felt as if we were not a legitimate church without one.

As we developed the use of our rented space in the mall, we progressed from serving free water bottles and coffee from a small coffee maker to operating a full-service coffee café. The vision for the café was to reach even more unchurched and de-churched people. People came, and we met them beyond the walls of a "normal" church. We met not just on Sundays but also during the week, listening to their concerns and offering help and prayer. The concept was good, the necessary leaders and resources emerged, and in 2009 we opened Overflow Coffee Café. This new space began to make a splash within the mall as a team of incredible volunteers from the church took on the mission. Unfortunately, the café did not garner enough business to justify the twenty thousand dollars invested in it. Nine months after it began, we closed the doors and waited. Sometimes God puts good things on hold for a more perfect time and place.

One reality of being a church without walls is learning to live in the tension between what you think God is doing and what he is actually doing. More often than not the direction we thought God was leading would take a sharp turn at some point. We were learning that these changes in direction were always for the better. The coffee café is a prime example of this, as we were able to donate the café and its equipment to the nonprofit organization we helped form: Overflow Christian Community Development Association (now known as Mosaic CCDA). Mosaic CCDA had an opportunity to lease a new facility next to a global corporation's new headquarters for just one dollar per month. God was upgrading the café we had envisioned, allowing this ministry to thrive and reach even more people than we had anticipated. Through all of this, we helped people see how the church is to operate without walls.

Today, the café is called Café Mosaic, and it's a thriving business in our community, living out the mission to reach people with Christ's love. The café focuses on building bridges in our community by creating jobs and providing job training. Its five core values are: (1) a loving atmosphere, (2) friendly faces, (3) excellent service, (4) steps to greatness, and (5) connecting conversations that are gospel-centered. Staff members engage their customers, getting to know them personally, which leads to great conversations about life, faith, and the hope found in Jesus. The café at the mall was a great beginning, but God positioned the new café, just three miles from its original location, as a strategic outpost of the church without walls in our community. It provides a much-needed space for people to relax and connect in the downtown area of our city. Many who used to avoid the area now consider Café Mosaic the perfect spot to gather.

The belief that the church is a building is one of Satan's greatest deceptions. When followers of Jesus accept that mentality, they miss the beauty of the most powerful organism on earth: Christ's bride, the church! The church is a new community, the people of God, filled with his Spirit and power. It is on the move throughout the world as his witnesses make disciples. There is nothing static about the church. Its architecture is composed not of buildings but of his people, who are the very temple of the living, eternal God. As the church lives up to this calling, it finds no barriers to block the view of Jesus. We follow his lead, and he is passionately and intentionally seeking his own—those lost, afraid, and hurting, who don't know they are loved and forgiven by him. Christ uses us to take his love to the world.

It is fascinating to read the entirety of Acts 17 and see how this process played out as Paul met people in the synagogues and marketplaces of his travels. Jesus abolished the established religious practices and began a brand new way, which he called "the church," the *ecclesia*. He gave the gift of his Holy Spirit, God dwelling in each believer, to lead them into truth. Overflow Church has done its best to operate with this mentality from the start. Originally, Jesus led us directly to the mall as our first office and gathering place. He had us begin our worship gatherings at the movie theater. Jesus showed the way for this during his own ministry, going beyond the walls of the church to the places where people lived. He is after hearts, and he leads us exactly to where they are. He continues to show us practical ways to break through doubt and unbelief with truth, grace, and love.

Consider what it means to you personally to be a church without walls. It may be time for you to remove the barriers you've been taught or put up in regard to church. Paul was violently zealous for his religious beliefs until he ran smack into Jesus. It set him free. Join Paul, Overflow, and the host of believers who embrace the true meaning of the church. Whether gathering together on Sunday for worship or engaging in the mission on other days of the week, go now and be the church!

Discussion Questions

1. When you think of the church, what comes to mind?

2. Read Acts 17:16–34. What do you notice about how Paul lived, taught, and engaged people both within and beyond the walls of the church?

3. What thoughts come to your mind as you reflect on Overflow's attempts to be a church without walls?

4. It's easy to get stuck in the mentality of going to church rather than being the church. What might help you remain active in living your faith beyond the walls?

5. If you were to rank yourself on a scale of one (ice cold) to ten (white hot), what ranking would you give your passion for going beyond the walls and being the church? What are the reasons for your ranking?

6. What steps can you take this week to put off the spectator mentality and be the church?

Then He said to them, "The harvest truly is great, but the laborers are few; therefore pray the Lord of the harvest to send out laborers into His harvest. Go your way; behold, I send you out as lambs among wolves. Carry neither money bag, knapsack, nor sandals; and greet no one along the road."

—Luke 10:2–4 NKJV

23

Where God Guides, He Provides

As the summer of 2009 approached, we had a growing sense that God had more in store for Overflow Church in the way of facilities and outreach. We were still renting space at the mall and movie theater, but we felt that a change of location might be his next direction. We'd been worshiping publicly for just over a year. We knew it was early to consider new arrangements, but we felt God's stirring. Our leadership team decided to submit our lives and perceived limitations to the truth of Matthew 6:33: "But seek first his kingdom and his righteousness, and all these things will be given to you as well." We determined our strategy would be to let God provide our next facility.

Little did we know the miracles God had in store for us or the lessons we would learn by seeking his kingdom first. In June the mall management announced that the Sears store would soon close. The loss of the Sears anchor-store complex would result in a huge loss of jobs. If felt like another defeat for our struggling community. I began driving to the facility often, praying in the parking lot for God to do something with that space that would be a blessing to our community. A few weeks later I shared with our leadership the growing burden I had to talk with the owners of the property and see what their plans were. Every step I took trying to locate the owner was a dead end. No one seemed to know who owned the property, which was strange because it had the largest footprint in the mall and included ten acres of parking.

As we continued to seek first his kingdom, one of our leaders and I took a whirlwind road trip to help a pastor friend in Brooklyn, New York. It was an incredible experience and included a miracle we needed to see. We helped my friend's church with an inner-city cleanup project to help create a children's playground. A forty-foot storage trailer on the property had to be rotated forty-five degrees to make it parallel with a larger building, thereby making space for the play area. The trailer lacked wheels and was completely full. Without a crane, this was an impossible task. Our small group of volunteers gathered and prayed that God would provide. As we said "Amen," the boom of a crane appeared across the street. We couldn't believe what we were seeing! We walked over and asked the workers on the adjacent construction site if they would help us move the trailer. We boldly asked, and they said yes! With the help of a large forklift and some creative driving, they moved the container to its new location so we could start the project. God moved both the trailer and our faith to a brand-new position! We knew that God was hearing us, and we could see that he was also present with us, working alongside.

After our return from this trip, God began to move as fast as I could follow. Through connections I had made with someone two years earlier, I found the father-son owners of the Sears property and asked to meet with them. The father wanted to hear my story, so I shared. Then he asked what we wanted. Were we seeking to lease, rent, or buy the property? I knew in my heart what God had told me to do, so I boldly asked if he and his son would donate the property to our little church. After all, if God could provide a crane, why not a property? This was no small thing—it was a 130,000-square-foot location worth millions of dollars.

The initial discussion with the owners went well but did not lead where I had hoped. We continued to apply Matthew 6:33, prayed, fasted, and waited to see what God would do. Five weeks later we were in the midst of creating the first coffee shop in our mall space, and we ran out of money to finish the project. Totally discouraged and desperate, I turned to God in complete dependence. At 6:45 a.m. on a Tuesday, I was driving to the post office and broke down in tears, crying out to God for help. Within minutes I was holding a check for ten thousand dollars, which had been sitting in our post office box. Just a few hours later, I received an e-mail from the owners of the Sears property, offering it to us as a donation. It was astounding! Where God guides, he provides.

If you grew up in or around church, you have likely heard a missionary share stories of God's miraculous provision. These stories strengthen our faith and encourage us to give generously to the work God is doing. Yet how often do they inspire us to live in faith and on mission in our own communities? In Luke 10, we read that Jesus sent the disciples out to experience the harvest, telling them to take nothing with them. They had to simply follow God where he led. The only preparation would be the teachings he had invested in them and the faith they had to follow him.

As a child I thought the missionaries' stories were cool, but not for me. I knew I didn't want to go overseas. Yet I did want to obey. God knew my heart, and it took some years to get me to the place of saying yes. He patiently brings us along. God wants to provide globally and locally through us in the same way. He will create new stories of provision in our lives. God wants us to boldly go into the harvest fields of our communities and trust him for every step of the journey. Where God guides, he truly does provide!

A memorable scene in the movie *Indiana Jones and the Last Crusade* depicts the hero taking a step of faith off the side of a cliff into what appears to be an abyss. He can see no bridge or anything to step on. The audience holds its breath as he steps off the edge, then breathes a sigh of relief as the bridge across the chasm becomes visible. In fact, it was there the entire time. This scene paints a great picture and parallels Luke 10. When we step out in faith to follow God, we can trust that he has already prepared the bridge, resources, people, or whatever is needed to move forward.

Overflow has found out firsthand that God is faithful as we walk with him. He does provide, and he does so generously in ways that give him great glory. As one person said, "God loves to show off huge for his kids when we believe him!" Have you considered that you may be missing God's generous provision by playing it safe? Push past the fear and trust him for the first step. As you take it, you will see him bless your obedience and show you the next move. One step at a time, you will experience your own stories of God's miraculous provision!

Discussion Questions

1. How have you seen God provide for you already in your life?

2. How do these memories encourage your faith? How might you use those stories to encourage others?

3. Have you had moments when you knew God was asking you to take a step of faith and trust him? What was that like? How did you respond?

4. Survey your life. How much of it is built around playing it safe and keeping things comfortable? How does your response relate to Luke 9? How does this challenge or encourage you?

5. What steps of faith do you need to take today to move forward with God on his mission and to experience his provision?

6. God is always ready to send us into his harvest field if we will follow him and respond with faith. What does this mean for your life today?

> But Jesus looked at them and said to them, "With men this is impossible, but with God all things are possible."
>
> —Matthew 19:26 NKJV

24

The Impossible Made Possible

During the first couple of years in our new community, I spent a lot of time meeting with community leaders and just listening. I was seeking to understand where God was at work and how he wanted us to engage in that work. We had a clear calling from the beginning that Overflow Church should be a blessing to our community. From the start, we lived our faith beyond the walls of the church. I met many leaders through the Christian Community Development Association (ccda.org), some of whom became mentors to me. I was excited to partner with whoever was doing development work in our community. However, by the time Overflow Church launched worship services in the movie theater, I realized that the specific type of organization I was looking for did not exist in our community. I had hoped to find a faith-based community development organization to partner with, but none could be found. I sheepishly approached Cindy and shared my growing passion to start a nonprofit focused on Christian community development. We both knew that to start both the church *and* a nonprofit would be crazy if God's hand was not in it.

Thankfully, what seemed completely impossible was made possible by God, who was light-years ahead of us in preparing the way. During our first year as a church, we were blessed to have an amazing lifelong resident and leader in the Benton Harbor community join us. Granny Rose, as we lovingly called her, became the prayer director at Overflow. Together we began to pray and discuss the idea of starting a Christian development agency. In August 2008, I felt led to give Rose my plane ticket and registration to the Christian Community Development Association's national conference being held in Miami. We could not afford two tickets, and I had a strong sense that she should be the one to go. I felt sure God could get me to Miami another time, which he did in 2013. Rose went to the conference and discovered the same vision I had. When she returned to Benton Harbor, we began gathering stakeholders, listening to discover the community's needs, finding funding, and forming the legal entity that became the Overflow Christian Community Development Association (as noted earlier, now known as Mosaic CCDA).

The process was long and daunting, unfolding over the next three years. Overflow Church was the catalyst to get things moving, but the Mosaic CCDA board of directors was composed of representatives from many different churches and organizations. We were following God's call to create a kingdom vehicle that would build bridges of collaboration and offer job creation and training in our community. From my survey of the community, I had noticed that the greatest need was for jobs and job training. One great challenge nonprofits face is finding sustainable funding. God gave me a vision for a new approach to funding that I call the "three streams" method. We built our nonprofit with funding from (1) social enterprises (non-for-profit businesses focused on social good and transformation), (2) grants, and (3) donors. Over the first six years of Mosaic CCDA's existence, we've watched God do the impossible by taking us from a volunteer-staffed organization with only 1,300 dollars in funding to a full-fledged Christian development association with more than forty full- and part-time employees and a budget of over 700,000 dollars. With God all things are possible.

I vividly remember the moment I shared this additional vision with my wife, Cindy. I knew God wanted Overflow to start a Christian development agency in our community. Yet I was apprehensive about the risk. I remember telling Cindy, "If God isn't in this, it is suicide to start two organizations at the same time." By God's grace we can look back and see that what seemed impossible on paper was possible because God authored it. That was Mary's experience in Luke 1 and reflects Jesus' teaching in Matthew 19:26. When God is involved, nothing is impossible. His ways are higher, his thoughts greater, and his plans are far more exciting than we can imagine. What he authors, he finishes!

Too often my limited imagination has placed a box around what God could do in my life, my work, my family, or my ministry. Is that true of you also? Have you considered that the Creator of the universe has far more resources than we can imagine? Science and technology continually advance, deepening our knowledge of creation. At the same time, this confirms how little we really know. God is the creator of all that exists, and he reigns supreme over it today. A life lived with and for him has endless possibilities because he is infinite. Everything exists by him and for him, and without him nothing exists. He has all we will ever need. Scripture states that our work for God results in his glory (see Heb. 13:20–21). And when God's glory is at stake, he always comes through! As we say at Overflow, "His story for his glory!"

If you have placed a box around God or your life with him, make a bold choice today. Blow the lid off the box and get rid of the walls! May your faith grow and the possibilities increase as you discover what it means to have the Creator of the universe as your financier, coach, leader, business partner and creative director. I pray you will move forward with a greater faith. Believe God can do the impossible in and through you. Let go of your fears and let him lead. You will discover that possibilities you never dreamed of come with saying yes to him.

Discussion Questions

1. How have you witnessed God doing seemingly impossible things in your life or in the lives of others?

2. Is there anything you are trusting God with that you have yet to see him do? Explain.

3. How might Overflow's story of God doing the "impossible" inform your perspective on your own situation?

4. What do you need to move forward with, even though it seems impossible? How does that inspire or challenge you?

5. Pray about your impossible situation, and consider your next steps in faith.

"He who has My commandments and keeps them, it is he who loves Me. And he who loves Me will be loved by My Father, and I will love him and manifest Myself to him."

—John 14:21 NKJV

25

Where Is God at Work?

As we moved through 2009, the financial realities of our small church and growing family weighed heavily on me. Many church planters must take secular employment to support their families, and that's exactly what I had to do. The first job I took was a community canvasser for the US Census Bureau. It's one thing to go door-to-door to invite people to church but entirely different to do so as a census worker, asking questions that are unwanted by most people. The experience was humbling, but I decided to make the best of it. As I did, I began to see God at work. On the first day, I filled my government-issued satchel with church brochures and volunteered to take all the addresses no one else wanted to go to. I prayed over homes and people as I walked the neighborhoods. Those who wanted to talk, I invited to visit Overflow at the theatre. Though it was a job I hadn't wanted, I could see that God was using it to expand awareness of his church and enlarge my view of our community—all while walking in the sunshine, which improved my health. Those days of walking my city enabled me to see people face-to-face, to see where and how they lived, and to become more aware of the needs pressing in on them.

When the Census Bureau job ended, I found a government-funded summer youth employment program, where I worked as a youth supervisor. The six-week program provided a daily introduction to the deeper issues the youth in our community face. Many had troubled lives and were trying to avoid more trouble by working during the summer. I was paired with a school security guard to supervise approximately sixteen youth, usually the most challenging students in the program. We showed them respect and taught them life skills, such as the value of working hard and doing their best. We listened to their challenges, and they gained a sense of accomplishment for a solid day of work. These interactions proved fruitful for the youth and for us. God was at work in significant ways in the lives of some of those teens, and he invited me to join him. He was already working; I just came alongside.

During this summer experience, I saw the power of respect, meaningful work, and a paycheck impact even the most difficult young people. One of our students had been expelled from school the previous year for fighting and seriously injuring another student. This troubled young person not only finished the program but also became a model student leader. Watching him interact with the other kids, and imagining the potential impact he could have, brought a new burden to my heart. I began to pray, believing God would show me his plan to sustain the success I'd witnessed that summer. The government grant might run out, but I was determined that the results I witnessed would not.

A few weeks later we developed the vision for Harbor Shine, a lawn-care and snowplowing service. Harbor Shine is a social enterprise operated by Mosaic CCDA that employs youth in the summer and adults throughout the year. Faithful as always, God brought us his plan exactly when we needed it. His plans are always perfect and precise, right down to putting me to work in the summer community program so I could see the potential for impacting our community by employing teens.

As Christ's followers, we must believe that God is alive and at work daily on the earth. This belief is the foundation supporting my heart and the work of Overflow Church. Henry Blackaby, in his *Experiencing God* study, describes this process: "When you see the Father at work around you, that is your invitation to adjust your life to him and join him in that work."[1] As I discovered through my employment experiences, this can lead us into situations we never would have chosen on our own. Yet we discover that we're exactly where the Father is working, and he asks us to join him. In John 14, Jesus commanded obedience from his disciples as an outflow of their love for him (see v. 15). The idea that God wanted to involve me in his work and that his only requirement was to love and obey him changed my life and ministry forever.

Jesus took this concept even further in John 14:21, when he said, "Whoever has my commands and keeps them is the who loves me. The one who loves me will be loved by my Father, and I too will love them and show myself to them." Jesus showed us the reciprocal relationship that occurs as we love and obey the Father. We love and obey, and he loves and gives even more of himself to us. What a beautiful picture of a life that overflows with the Father. When we love God, he pours into us. When we obey him, we pour ourselves out in the places he shows us, and as a result he pours even more of himself into us.

I pray that you will be encouraged as you look for the places God may be at work around you. Is your love for him great enough to obey and follow him into the work he is already doing? He wants you to be part of it. It's an exciting adventure, and I hope you will move forward with a heart filled with love for God.

Discussion Questions

1. Where do you see God at work around you right now?

2. Have you considered that God extends an invitation for you to join him in what he is doing? How does that inspire or challenge you?

3. How does the idea that love leads to obedience impact the way you see your relationship with God?

4. What would you like to see happen over the next few months with your love for God and your corresponding obedience? What practical steps could you take to grow in both?

5. Is there anything you know God is inviting you to be a part of, but you've been disobedient or delayed your obedience? What are the reasons for that?

6. Are you ready for the adventure of letting God fill you for what he has while you pour yourself out for those he shows you? What does your next step look like?

Note

1. Henry T. Blackaby and Claude V. King, *Experiencing God: Knowing and Doing the Will of God*, workbook (Nashville: LifeWay, 1990), 64.

PART 6

Being Leads to Doing

My dear brothers and sisters, take note of this: Everyone should be quick to listen, slow to speak and slow to become angry.

—James 1:19

26

Personal Transformation through Listening

I first heard the phrase "Being leads to doing" in 2005 while studying at Fuller Seminary. As my classmates and I discussed the concept, we began to see how much of our lives and leadership were focused on what we did for God. It was a breakthrough moment when I realized that God is more concerned with who I am becoming than with what I have done for him. It was freeing to grasp that life with Christ centered on receiving what God had for me and that fruitfulness would follow. I no longer felt the need to drive myself to achieve for God. Instead, I was motivated to know God and watch him work in and through me. I would love to say I have mastered this, but he's still teaching me this

lesson today. In fact, after just a few years of church planting, I slipped back into attempting to achieve something for
God while giving little attention to who I was becoming.

After a time, I noticed that something about my person-
ality and leadership style was negatively affecting others.
More than once, fellow leaders at Overflow left my office
in tears of frustration, and I sensed a change in the way my
wife felt about our marriage. During that season of high
stress, I was trying to achieve more than God had asked of
me, and I became a poor listener who dispensed too much
"helpful" advice to others. I had become slow to listen, quick
to speak, and even quicker to become angry. My strong
defensive posture kept others at a distance. Realizing there
was a problem, Cindy and I decided to seek help from a marriage counselor. The first couple of sessions seemed to go
well, but on the third visit the counselor suggested I read a
book on anger, and added that it would be a great help in both
our marriage and ministry. That moment, and that book, was
a wake-up call for me. As I worked through the pages of the
book, God began to soften, teach, and transform me.

While I'm still very much in process, God has begun a
deep, transformative work in me. I've been told more
recently that I'm an excellent listener, and I know that only
God could accomplish that change. He has used the people
in my life to teach me to listen and to find new ways of

loving them, especially my wife. This transformation in *being* has made me far more effective in *doing*. God continues to help me listen to him first, then lead others. I recall Peter, who just wasn't getting the picture on the Mount of Transfiguration. God spoke from heaven and said, "This is My beloved Son. Hear Him!" (Luke 9:35 NKJV). I'm definitely learning to listen!

The second important lesson God taught me through that season was that anger was often my reaction to situations that were out of my control. Many things in my life, then and now, are beyond my control, but my response to that reality is different now. The apostle Paul taught in Ephesians 4 that anger itself is not a sin, but what is done in anger can be. During that season of my life, God showed me how to trust him in a deeper way, giving to him the things I couldn't control. These were vital lessons as I reached out to the community in ways that often took me far beyond my ability to control—whether it was the people, events, or situations I encountered.

God is faithful and in control. When we let him transform us, greater works result. I can't imagine what would have happened if I'd been resistant to the personal transformation I so desperately needed. After humbling myself to accept the truth, I was set free.

Have you ever had someone lovingly correct you about a blind spot in your life? Is there anyone in your life who can ask you tough questions and point out your need to change? Part of the Christian life is choosing not to walk alone. Yes, Christ is with us, and so are the brothers and sisters in the church family. Members of the church are to act and respond to each other as parts of a body, Christ's body (see 1 Cor. 12:27). Our collective job is to sharpen, encourage, and spur on one another to become more like Christ (see Prov. 27:17; Eph. 4:11–13; Heb. 10:24–25). The hand reaches down to help tie the shoe that protects the foot. The eye guides the hand. Jesus wants us to work together for the good of the whole, just as the parts of a body do.

I realized that I needed to grow as a listener and deal with anger in my life. In order to do that, I had to first listen to others. It has been said that we have two ears and one mouth so we will listen twice as much as we talk. Quietly listening to God and others brings great insight that leads to spiritual breakthroughs. Listening doesn't always come naturally, and much of modern life is filled with noise. But as we learn to listen well, we will experience more of God and the life he intends for us.

Discussion Questions

1. Review the Scriptures listed in this chapter. What are you learning about how members of a Christian community should relate to one another?

2. Who are the people in your life who can ask hard questions and point out your blind spots? Describe an occasion when that took place.

3. If you don't have people in your life who can speak candidly to you, what steps do you need to take to correct that?

4. What is your plan for listening and dealing with anger with the people identified above?

5. How would you rate yourself as a listener from one to ten (one being poor and ten being great)? Explain. Name some practical ways to work on your skills as a listener, both to God and others.

6. On a scale of one to ten, rate yourself on handling anger (one being poor and ten being great). Explain. What can you do to let God have greater control in your life and lessen your anger in the days ahead?

For I know the thoughts that I think toward you, says the LORD, thoughts of peace and not of evil, to give you a future and a hope.

—Jeremiah 29:11 NKJV

27

The Space Between

There is a space in everyone's life between their dreams and reality. Anytime we begin something new, we have a sense of anticipation. We envision how our lives, and the lives of our loved ones, will be better as a result of these new endeavors. We may realize that it won't happen overnight, but we do expect things to be better in the future than they were in the past. We launch out boldly, but we often forget about that space in-between—the distance between aspiration and realization. As a result, we are unprepared for the challenges, trouble, grief, and opportunities to grow that we encounter before we reach our destinations. In 2009 and 2010, Overflow was living in that space between, and the discouragement and pressure were mounting.

We had launched the church, formed Mosaic CCDA, and received the donation of the Sears property. In my mind, we'd entered the Promised Land and were about to experience the blessings of God. We were on the journey toward the fulfillment of our God-given dreams. Then came the space between, a place God used to prepare us for what would come next. It was during this time period that Cindy and I almost lost our home before selling it on a short sale, and the church was handed litigation and a cease and desist order regarding the donated property. For me, this was an incredibly dark time that brought deep discouragement and doubts like I'd never experienced before. In retrospect I see that God was growing my faith during this season. At the time, however, I just wanted it to be over. A wise mentor helped me understand that the space between was exactly where God wanted me. Going through that time was the only way to develop more of Jesus' character in me, which I would need for the next season.

I would love to say this advice helped me adjust quickly and embrace this time of uncertainty, but it was a daily struggle. I began to read 2 Corinthians 4:7–11 and ponder it daily: "But we have this treasure in earthen vessels, that the excellence of the power may be of God and not of us.

We are hard-pressed on every side, yet not crushed; we are perplexed, but not in despair; persecuted, but not forsaken; struck down, but not destroyed—always carrying about in the body the dying of the Lord Jesus, that the life of Jesus also may be manifested in our body. For we who live are always delivered to death for Jesus' sake, that the life of Jesus also may be manifested in our mortal flesh" (NKJV). As I read these verses, a new understanding of my circumstances erupted in me. I was being pressed into the image of Jesus— and it hurt! But I was encouraged to think that a new season was coming, and I began to embrace the space between.

I was also able to share this lesson with others in similar seasons of difficulty. We found we could encourage one another and find God together in the space between. Since that time, Overflow has moved through other such seasons, and understanding the reality of the space between gives us endurance as we watch our hopes and dreams come into being. We are learning to embrace rather than avoid that space because it is a necessary part of our journey with God.

Jeremiah 29:11 is often printed on greeting cards or used as wall art. The verse is inspiring and a great source of encouragement. However, we usually overlook the context of the verse, Jeremiah 29:4–14, which describes the situation the people of Israel were living in. They were captives in the foreign land of Babylon. They were afraid and unsure how to live. God spoke through Jeremiah, telling them to continually seek the peace of their captors and the city where they'd been taken. They were to believe God still had a future and hope for them, despite their circumstances. Talk about a space between! Often we believe God has a purpose for us, but we don't want to go through the uncomfortable, painful, and downright hard things that lie between us and his goal. The space between is the chisel and hammer God uses to shape us into the image of his Son.

Joseph was a young man with a bold dream for a bright future. However, as his story unfolded, he found himself thrown in a pit, then put in prison, and only years later elevated as a ruler in the palace (see Gen. 37–50). Joseph learned a deep dependency on God and the kind of character that would allow God to trust Joseph with not only a position of power but ultimately the influence and stewardship of two nations (Egypt and Israel). What God taught him through the process was priceless and could only be learned by going through the space between. No matter your situation today, you can trust that God is working out his plan. With God, every season has a reason. The spaces between are his precision tools to shape God's dreams and our destinies.

Whether you are in a season of dreaming, difficulty, or destiny, give God the glory and enjoy the journey. There are always gaps in life, places where we wonder what God is doing. Those gaps are where God does his best work. May you embrace the season you are in and allow the space between to mold you to be more like Jesus.

Discussion Questions

1. Are you in a season of dreaming, difficulty, or destiny? Explain.

2. What is God trying to teach you in this season? How is he making you more like Jesus? Are you able to see how he is preparing you for your destiny? How so?

3. Do you believe that God has hope and a great future for you? What steps do you need to take to grow in your faith and move forward with God?

4. Read Ecclesiastes 3:1–13. Take note of how these verses describe timing, seasons, and the space between. What do you learn from this passage?

5. Ecclesiastes 3:9–11 shows us that God makes everything beautiful in his timing and that we are to do good in each season. Do you trust that God will make your situation beautiful in his timing? Why or why not? How can you take joy and do good in this season, regardless of what you are going through?

And when they could not come near Him because of the crowd, they uncovered the roof where He was. So when they had broken through, they let down the bed on which the paralytic was lying. When Jesus saw their faith, He said to the paralytic, "Son, your sins are forgiven you."

—Mark 2:4–5 NKJV

28

Simply Profound

In the early days of Overflow Church, we had an opportunity to help out at a local homeless shelter. One of the program directors at the shelter attended the church and mentioned the existing needs. Beyond the obvious needs for food, clothing, and shelter, this staff member saw spiritual needs in the homeless people there. She suggested I go and teach at their large gathering. The shelter hosted a monthly meal and celebration for alumni and friends in an effort to build community, connect people, and help their graduates continue to progress in life. Other churches and organizations would supply the meal and activities for children; my role was to share Jesus in a way that would give hope.

I was very excited about this opportunity but totally unprepared for how this simple gathering would profoundly impact each of us that night. Upon arriving at the event, I was encouraged to see more than seventy-five adults and nearly fifty children present. The meal and children's activities were great fun, and a true spirit of joy was evident. The majority of the group was African American, and they displayed a beautiful spirit of inclusion toward me and the few other Caucasians who were there. Each participant was either homeless or had been in the past. The latter served as a great encouragement to those in the shelter. We witnessed community as I believe it is meant to be, occurring because of the presence of Christ at work outside of the walls of the church.

When it was time for me to speak about Christ, I was introduced as a volunteer who would teach about "life skills." I didn't know what to expect from the group. The normal meeting space in the basement of the shelter was being renovated and not available for use. As a result, I was set up to speak with a whiteboard perched atop a washing machine in their small laundry room. However, this wasn't just any laundry room; it was a tiny corner of their "Michigan basement." If you have lived in Michigan, you know that means a damp, dark, subterranean room with a dirt floor. It was a truly humble space God gave me to share

Jesus with these new friends. Nearly everyone who had attended the dinner crammed into the laundry room, around the corner, and up the stairwell to hear about Jesus. I felt as if we were back in the days of the early church, meeting in the upper rooms (or in this case, lower rooms!) of houses.

I shared about my own struggles in life and the hope I have found in Jesus. The message had a profound impact as people responded to the gospel and prayed for one another's needs. From that small beginning, our partnership with the shelter has blossomed. We now provide transportation every Sunday for people from the shelter who want to be part of Overflow Church. Our fellowship has been enlarged, blessing our lives as well as theirs. The impact of that one night has been profound as we have grown to love the families, been loved by some of them, and learned from them through their trying situations. We have also witnessed a handful over the years who have decided to follow Jesus and serve him with their gifts at the church and in the community. When we are faithful in the most humble of circumstances, God will do incredible things.

Jesus lived an intentionally simple life and humbly ministered to those around him. The religious and political leaders of the day totally missed or dismissed what Jesus was doing, and we often do too. His way of doing things seems humble and even humiliating. God still works in very simple, humble, yet profound ways. He said that he would confound the wise and use the simple (see 1 Cor. 1:27). That first night at the shelter, simply sharing a meal and talking about Jesus in a musty basement, made a profound impact on my life and on Overflow. It changed our concept of outreach and opened our eyes to see the potential right around us. This weekly outreach is still taking place more than seven years after that one event.

In Mark 2:4–5, we see that people crowded around Jesus' to hear his teaching. Though there was no more space for people to enter, the simple, humble, and profound faith of a few men led them to break through the roof in order get their sick friend to Jesus. When I taught that night at the shelter, I witnessed the faith of many as people tried to break through and make room to hear more about Jesus. I thought of this incident in Mark 2 and what it must have been like to be in that house when the roof suddenly opened up. I couldn't help but draw a parallel to that amazing night, sharing Jesus' love with new friends. No doubt we would all love to share the gospel in a beautiful, spacious room with perfect tech equipment and other resources available. But that wasn't important to Jesus. For him, open hearts and eager minds were the perfect setting for teaching about the love of God—regardless of where he found them. Jesus has promised to lead us just as completely as his Father led him. The shelter helped me tune in to a whole new frequency of listening to Jesus, following him into profound and unexpected places that are ready for the gospel.

Discussion Questions

1. Have you ever considered how simple and humble yet profound Jesus' ways are? What comes to mind as you think about his ministry?

2. Have you ever seen someone sharing the gospel and thought either they or their methods were too simple to be blessed by God? Based on your learning in this chapter, how do you now view that circumstance?

3. Do you ever feel that some situations or people are beneath you and not worth your time? Where do you think this thought comes from?

4. If you had been there when the men opened the roof to bring their friend to Jesus, what do you think would have been running through your mind? Explain.

5. What are a few practical ideas that might help you slow down to see Jesus work in simple, humble ways to impact your church or community?

6. The paralytic man had friends with a simple, humble, and profound faith. Do you have those kinds of friends? Are you that kind of friend? What would it take to cultivate that simple faith in you and in your circle of friends?

And may the Lord make your love for one another and for all people grow and overflow, just as our love for you overflows.

—1 Thessalonians 3:12 NLT

29

Relationships Redefined

Reconciliation. Redistribution. Relocation. Those "3 Rs" are the core philosophy of the Christian Community Development Association (ccda.org), taught for decades by Dr. John Perkins. Each R is central to the gospel and to Jesus' life and ministry. When we come into close contact with Jesus, our relationships with him and with our neighbors are redefined. As a church that was learning a great deal about reaching into our community with Christ's love, we came to embrace the 3 Rs as defining characteristics.

First comes reconciliation. God reconciles us to himself, then calls us to serve as ambassadors of reconciliation to others. This new love from God begins vertically, then redefines our relationships horizontally. Next is redistribution. God has called each of us to a life of good stewardship and generosity. As we embrace this, we realize we are blessed in order to be a blessing. We begin to redistribute our resources and relationships. Finally, there is relocation. Some would say Jesus relocated by moving from heaven to earth (see John 1:14). As we embrace the life of Jesus, we become willing to relocate in order to live as he did. Historically, the Christian Community Development Association has viewed this as physically relocating to live among the poor in our cities. While I don't believe God requires that of everyone, it was exactly what God called my family and that of eight others to do. We relocated into the heart of our city (see Neh. 11:1–2).

After a few years of living out the 3 Rs, we began to see both the blessing and the burden in this lifestyle. The blessing came as we made new friends, saw resources shared, and discovered a new appreciation for those we now called neighbors. The burden came as we saw some leave our community. Many of those we had loved and labored with experienced God's call to a new season of life in a different city or state. At first Cindy and I didn't talk much about that; but as time went on and more and more relationships were redefined, we began to articulate the toll it was taking. It seemed that as soon as we began to really love someone, they would leave, plunging us into another cycle of grief. We called this our "revolving door," but the term doesn't do justice to the pattern of relational loss we were experiencing.

As the revolving door continued to spin, we talked to others and consulted God's Word for guidance. We gained a new perspective that helped us understand the roles each person played in a particular season of God's kingdom work. While we still wanted everyone to stay, we learned to grieve the loss while trusting that God's hand was on the process. People were being brought into and taken out of our lives to fulfill strategic purposes, both for them and for our community. As we release those who leave into God's plan for them, he wants us to cherish the beautiful people he allows to remain among us for a longer term. He has helped us focus our attention and energy on building these relationships. This has proven invaluable to our family. We have learned to fully engage in the present, to live in the now—with whoever is among us. We love completely and hold loosely so God is able to do as he sees fit.

The heart of the gospel is God's love for us and his desire to restore us to relationship with him, his creation, and each other. The challenges of daily living keep us from experiencing that reality in many ways. The 3 Rs call us to redefine our relationships according to God's desire. We're challenged to reconcile with him and others, to relocate so that we live where he would want us to be, and to redistribute our resources generously as he asks. Any of these three acts, done in isolation, would be daunting. To live by this philosophy, we need God's love and guidance flowing into our lives. As the apostle Paul put it, "May the Lord make your love for one another and for all people grow and overflow, just as our love for you overflows" (1 Thess. 3:12 NLT). Only through a vibrant, growing relationship with Jesus can we be so consistently filled with love that it overflows to those around us through reconciliation, redistribution, and relocation.

This kind of living will hurt. We experienced that at Overflow. And the early church experienced it as believers moved outward to spread the gospel. They faced persecution, separation, and other hardships. Transition will be a constant in our communities as God moves people in and out for his kingdom's sake. Our modern lifestyle of mobility brings pain, but we must continue to engage in reconciling relationships. As we do, we will find the beauty in each person and enjoy the fruit they bring during our time together. We may not always see the results we hoped for, but we know that God is faithful through the seasons of life. Reconciliation, redistribution, and relocation—the 3 Rs bring God's love to our cities, and the fruit that results will remain. Some of it will be seen locally, some of it will be seen in our lifetime, but most of it will be seen elsewhere and in eternity.

Discussion Questions

1. Read 1 Thessalonians 3:12. How does this verse speak to your life today?

2. Have you practiced any of the 3 Rs in your life? What was it like? What was the result?

3. Which of the 3 Rs do you find most challenging? Why?

4. What action would you need to take to implement one or more of the Rs in your life? Commit it to writing.

5. How have you responded to transitions with people you loved due to relocation or life-stage changes?

6. What would you say to someone who is grieving over the loss of or change in a relationship due to a relocation or other act of obedience to God?

7. Paul alluded to the seasons of life in 1 Corinthians 3:6 when he spoke of each person's role in God's work: "I planted the seed, Apollos watered it, but God has been making it grow." What is your current role in life, ministry, and church?

> What does it profit, my brethren, if someone says he has faith but does not have works? Can faith save him? If a brother or sister is naked and destitute of daily food, and one of you says to them, "Depart in peace, be warmed and filled," but you do not give them the things which are needed for the body, what does it profit?
>
> —James 2:14–16 NKJV

30

More Than Words

Mission statements have been popular in leadership circles over the past couple of decades, and that has led to better organizational clarity. However, clarity doesn't always lead to action, and some mission statements are nothing more than words posted on a wall. At Overflow Church, we have been determined that our mission statement will be something more than words. Over the last few years, our mission statement has taken on a life of its own. It states, "Overflow exists to reach the unchurched and de-churched in our world, journeying together as we learn how to passionately follow Jesus and joyfully serve others."

This statement is reinforced each and every week through our benediction, which is a reminder to "Go now and be the church!" It has been exciting to watch the myriad of ways that mission happens week after week and year after year. Our people have taken this to heart as a daily call to action.

In the early days of Overflow, many service teams from other churches came to help us with short-term outreach projects in our community. We hosted fifty-five of these teams, harnessing their passion, resources, and time to bless our neighborhoods. As a small church, we were not always able to meet our neighbors' needs on our own, but by partnering with these service teams, we multiplied our impact. With their help, we painted houses, made home repairs, and cleaned up parks. Within a short time, many people attending the church began offering to do the same kinds of things the service teams were doing. We were no longer the "baby church" that needed help along the way. We were growing up and taking on the responsibility of nurturing our community.

One of my favorite memories of the transition from depending on service teams to mobilizing our own people took place when we moved into our first stand-alone church home. In the spring of 2012, a youth service team came to help us paint, clean, and landscape the property. They were a great blessing, and their help arrived at just the right time. When they left, members of the local high school football team came to help us, and they were joined by volunteers from our church. It was exciting to see our people joining with the football players and coaches to paint the building. We were beginning to journey together and joyfully serve Jesus in new ways. Today, God continues to build a community as people put their faith into action, ensuring that our mission statement and weekly benediction are more than just words.

One of the challenges all believers face is to make our walk match our talk. The world around us is listening and watching, and it often finds a gap between our words and our actions. Many label Christians as hypocrites because we do not always live out what we profess. If that is true in your life, allow the Holy Spirit to convict and challenge you. He will lead you further into his presence and into authentic Christian living. Conviction is his gentle nudge. He loves you very much and wants your faith to be authentic and full of life. Accept his counsel, guidance, and comfort as you make your faith more than mere words.

When we put our faith into action, God will use even the smallest things in big ways. Little becomes big with our God! What is in your path today, or, better yet, who? Put Christ's love into action; it could make an exponential difference. A small pebble thrown into a body of still water will create a large ripple. As James said, it is not enough simply to tell someone, "Be warmed and filled"; we must respond with action (see 2:14–16). God will show you what needs to be done and how to do it. Sometimes that will be something you do privately. At other times it will involve partnership with others. I pray you are able to see how to put love into action so your faith will not just make a ripple but a tidal wave!

Discussion Questions

1. Read James 2:14–16 and reflect on it. What do these verses say to you and your life today?

2. Would you say you are putting your faith into action in your daily life? If so, what "ripples" have you seen? If not, why not?

3. Can you identify any recent occasions when your faith has amounted to just words? What can you do to correct that?

4. Is there any situation or person you need to respond to with faith-filled action? Who might partner with you in that?

5. How has God spoken to you through the stories and Scriptures in this chapter? With whom can you share this lesson today?

PART 7

Bridges Built by Faith

He said to him, "What is written in the law? What is your reading of it?" So he answered and said, "'You shall love the Lord your God with all your heart, with all your soul, with all your strength, and with all your mind,' and 'your neighbor as yourself.'" And He said to him, "You have answered rightly; do this and you will live." But he, wanting to justify himself, said to Jesus, "And who is my neighbor?"

—Luke 10:26–29 NKJV

31

Who Is My Neighbor?

The question "Who is my neighbor?" was first posed by a lawyer to Jesus (Luke 10:29). Jesus responded with the story of a Samaritan who helped a Jewish man who had been robbed, beaten, and left to die by the roadside. Others passed by the wounded man but kept moving, even going out of their way to avoid him. He was a Samaritan, a man despised by the Jews of his day because of his race, ethnicity, and religion and who became the hero simply by showing kindness to the hurting man. Through this simple tale, Jesus taught that our neighbors are any persons we encounter, no matter who they are: similar or different, friend or foe.

When Cindy and I moved our family into Benton Harbor, we were the only white family in the neighborhood, and we stood out, to say the least. We not only had a different skin color but also brought a new approach to daily life and neighboring. Our young children played in the backyard every day. Cindy began to share chips and soda with adults and popsicles with kids, and I looked for ways to bless others by serving them.

We didn't have much to work with from a material standpoint, but we had a God-given love for our neighbors. With that we began to build bridges. One of the first bridges was to our next-door neighbor. Cindy simply asked if she liked Squirt, the lemon-lime soft drink. That can of Squirt led to hours of conversation in our backyard and a new friendship. Our young neighbor proceeded to share her life story and some of the difficulties she faced growing up in a community mired in poverty and crime. Today, her story is still unfolding, and our lives are still connected. All that began with a simple act of hospitality.

We chose to live in a neighborhood that others regularly avoided and, because we did, many good things happened. One day a service team from another church called me to ask if they could come and paint a house in our community. I was excited because God had put it on my heart to help our neighbor with her home someday. The day came quickly and with great joy as I asked if she would like her house painted. She said yes, but expected a catch. She asked what paperwork she would have to fill out. She was overjoyed when I said, "None! All you have to do is pick out the color." She had wanted to paint her house for twenty-five years but hadn't been able to afford it. When the house painting was completed, she came over to greet me in the driveway as I returned home from work. She was carrying a casserole as a gift for our family, along with a tearful apology and hug. She told me that when we moved into the neighborhood, she did not want her children or grandchildren near us because of the color of our skin, but she now realized that we loved Jesus just as she did and saw us as a part of her extended family. The casserole turned out to be one of the best I'd ever had. Loving our neighbors was having a greater impact on them, and us, than we'd ever imagined.

Although I am only in my thirties, I have seen the concept of community erode during my lifetime. I have seen it move from the openness of the front porch to the seclusion of the back deck, from the intimacy of hand-written letters to the superficiality of 140-character tweets, from family scrapbooks to Snapchat, and from friends you like to spend time with to friends you "like" on Facebook. There is no doubt that we are more "connected" than ever through electronic media, yet we are more personally isolated than we have ever been. As George Gallup Jr. said, "We are physically detached from each other. We change places of residence frequently. One survey revealed that seven in ten Americans do not know their neighbors. As many as one-third of Americans admit to frequent periods of loneliness."[1]

When I look back to my previous, suburban neighborhood, I realize that I knew very few of my neighbors. It took intentional effort over the last eight years for Cindy and me to get to know our neighbors in our new community, and we still have quite a ways to go. As Jesus said, we are to love God and love our neighbors (see Matt. 22:37–39). That takes effort. To do it, you must be willing to walk across the street, reach across the fence, offer a helping hand, or even just say hello.

Our world is desperate for community and is once again asking the question "Who is my neighbor?" Though many people may not realize it, they have been created in the image of a God who lives in Trinitarian community (see Gen. 1:26–27). We are designed to live in community with others. Yet how many of us actually experience community? At the core of our faith is God's redemptive plan to restore humanity to fellowship with himself and others (see 2 Cor. 5:12–21). Christ himself has created a community, his body, the church—a community of people from every nation on the planet. Through the presence of the Holy

Spirit, we are united by his love and grace, which destroys all barriers between us (see Eph. 2:11–22). When someone asked Jesus, "Who is my neighbor?" he astounded those listening by redefining the term. Your neighbor is anyone God puts in your path, whether they are like you or not. May this truth help you create new community through Jesus Christ. Embrace your neighbors with his love!

Discussion Questions

1. Who are your neighbors? List those who live in your neighborhood, the top ten people you spend the most time with, and at least ten people who regularly cross your path.

2. What do you notice about this list? What does God want you to notice about this list?

3. What steps would you need to take to know your neighbors? What space in your schedule would you need to make in order to love them?

4. Reread the story of the Samaritan in Luke 10. What stands out to you?

5. What action will you take based on your discoveries about the meaning of loving your neighbor? When will you take them?

Note

1. George Gallup Jr., *The People's Religion* (New York: Macmillan, 1989), quoted in Randy Frazee, *The Connecting Church: Beyond Small Groups to Authentic Community* (Grand Rapids, MI: Zondervan, 2001), 5.

"Steep your life in God-reality, God-initiative, God-provisions. Don't worry about missing out. You'll find all your everyday human concerns will be met. Give your entire attention to what God is doing right now, and don't get worked up about what may or may not happen tomorrow. God will help you deal with whatever hard things come up when the time comes."

—Matthew 6:30–34 MSG

32

Stay Focused and He Will Provide

Faith grows as it's exercised, just as muscles do. As we live by faith, God guides and blesses us, and before long we have more faith than we thought possible. That is what happened in Overflow Church as we built relational bridges in our community. We sought God's plan for moving out of the movie theater and into a permanent building. Our hope was to have an active presence in the community, building relationships with Christ at the center seven days a week. In the fall of 2009, we learned, after four months of prayer and trusting God's promise in Matthew 6:33–34, that all 130,000 square feet of the former Sears store would be donated to our church.

This was truly a miracle, and we praised God for it. Yet we knew that we must exercise due diligence as well. In a whirlwind ninety-day period, we did the investigative work to determine the feasibility of taking ownership of that commercial property, all the while still planting the church, establishing Mosaic CCDA, and finishing the coffee café in the mall. During this hectic time, I was determined to keep my focus on God. I knew that only his grace, wisdom, and guidance would bring us through. During the due diligence process, we engaged a commercial HVAC contractor, a commercial architect, a commercial roofing company, a building committee, lawyers, environmental consultants, and financial advisors to assess our situation. We were blessed to have a multitude of wise counselors, and God used them each in mighty ways.

After hearing from our many consultants, we determined that we could accept the donation only if two conditions were met: (1) The outstanding financial obligations attached to the property (approximately sixty thousand dollars) must be met by the donor; and (2) the donor would have to indemnify us from any future legal actions taken by the owner of the adjacent property (a mall). Our goal was to position our church well for the future and protect us from financial liability. Little did we know at the time, but those two simple conditions would position our church to endure two and a half years without the ability to use the location and legal fees totaling more than a hundred thousand dollars. If it was not for the two conditions and their corresponding provision, we would not have been able to withstand the financial toll of being without the property during the litigation. God had taught us an important lesson. Focus on him, and he will provide. The bridges God built during this season continue to bring rewards to this day.

One of my favorite memories during this time of waiting had to do with a gas bill of six thousand dollars for the vacant, unused Sears property. We couldn't afford to pay the bill. Through the negotiations of a friend, we were able to get the next bill reduced to three thousand dollars, but we still couldn't afford it. I walked into the building one January day and boldly did something by faith. I turned off all the heat and placed a garden thermometer near the light panel. I simply prayed, "God this is your property, and we cannot afford to heat it so the pipes won't crack. I am asking that you keep it at forty degrees for the winter. In Jesus' name. Amen." I walked out of the building trusting God for a miracle. I went back at least every other day for the next three months to check the temperature. Only once did the dial on that little garden thermometer move below forty degrees—for one day, to 39.5! God had provided once again, and to this day I keep that little thermometer as a reminder of what God is able to do when we have faith.

When the leadership team at Overflow Church knew it was time to move out of the movie theater and find a more permanent home, rather than moving impulsively, we chose to pray and study Matthew 6:30–34 for ninety days. By the end of the summer, God had proven himself more than faithful by providing the miraculous donation of the Sears property, which later produced the resources needed to purchase our first stand-alone building. God is true to his word and will provide if we let go of worry and stay focused on him.

We usually want to control things, to have our lives neatly organized and figured out. It's natural that we want to know where our next meals will come from or how we will provide clothes and housing for our families. Yet Jesus' teaching in Matthew 6 flips our natural inclination upside down. Jesus showed us that to follow him is to enter into a new reality, an abundant life where worry about position or provision is unnecessary. To walk with God is to trust him to provide you with his very best. When we pay attention to God in every aspect of our lives, we see him provide not just material things but love, wisdom, and innovation as well. We miss these things when we try to maintain control. God is waiting for you to quit worrying, to let go of your need to figure it out and just follow him. When you do, you will see God do the seemingly impossible to take care of you, his child. He loves you and, yes, you can trust him with your life.

Discussion Questions

1. Does the story of Overflow Church trusting God to provide for all its needs—including the donation of a location—seem too good to be true? Explain.

2. Do you tend to worry when you cannot control things in your daily life? How does this chapter speak to you today?

3. What would happen for you if you spent the next thirty days applying the truth of Matthew 6:30–34 to your life?

4. Do you believe God will provide for you when you focus on him? Why or why not?

5. How does it challenge or encourage you to hear that you can trust God with your whole life?

6. What big issue or need do you have today that you could take to God?

7. Memorize Matthew 6:33–34 this week and begin trusting God in deeper ways.

Then He said, "Go out, and stand on the mountain before the LORD." And behold, the LORD passed by, and a great and strong wind tore into the mountains and broke the rocks in pieces before the LORD, but the LORD was not in the wind; and after the wind an earthquake, but the LORD was not in the earthquake; and after the earthquake a fire, but the LORD was not in the fire; and after the fire a still small voice.

—1 Kings 19:11–12 NKJV

33

Hearing God's Voice

In January 2010, I experienced a miraculous move of God. As mentioned earlier, God had led me to ask the owners of a 130,000-square-foot commercial store and the 10.5 acres of land that composed the Sears property at the local mall to donate it to Overflow Church. And they did! The process of receiving this donation was marked by many challenges, but God prevailed, and I entered 2010 on a spiritual mountaintop. Our leadership team had decided to have its first twenty-one-day fast at the start the year as a way to center ourselves and hear from God at the beginning of what promised to be a new and exciting season in the church's life. For a church of around one hundred people, this building was evidence that God had moved a major mountain. During the fast, I was able to get away for a five-day prayer retreat at a small cabin in the woods. This retreat proved to be critical for dealing with the next mountain—one that was about to land right on top of us.

My days at the cabin were an incredible time of solitude, Sabbath, and silence, intertwined with prayer, fasting, reading, and exercise. My physical health was restored, and my soul was filled in new ways. God was pouring into me the strength and wisdom I would need for the season he knew was coming. During my time at the cabin, I gained a greater recognition of and belief in the fact that God is with me. The reality of his presence in my life is far more important than any challenge or circumstance I may face, and God reminded me of this in significant ways. I did not know what would be waiting for me when I returned home, but he did. I entered that challenge knowing that he would be with me every step of the way.

I returned to our community knowing that the God who moved mountains had met me on the "mountaintop." It did not take long for reality to hit me, though, as I stopped by the post office on my way into town and found a cease and desist order from the township, telling us we could not use our new property. About two weeks later, a sheriff's deputy served notice of a lawsuit against Overflow, delivered to our office in the presence of some volunteers. God had moved a mountain all right, and I felt as if it had fallen on top of me. The pain and confusion we experienced was profound, but we sensed the God of the impossible was present with us. We had heard God before and had confidence we would continue to hear him in the days ahead.

A twenty-one-day corporate fast and a personal prayer retreat may not sound exciting to some and even crazy to others. It is important to understand the motive behind them. As mentioned earlier, Overflow Church is called to be a "new wineskin" (see Luke 5), a church that communicates the gospel in new and innovative ways. Jesus' teaching on new wineskins describes a time when his disciples would fast in order to have "new wine" poured in. Our goal is to do just that—to set aside time amid the busyness of life to seek and hear him. When God speaks, it produces a "mountaintop" experience. Matthew 17 relates a similar mountaintop, the Mount of Transfiguration, where Peter, James, and John witnessed Jesus transfigured along with Moses and Elijah. Peter was so excited that he wanted to pitch a tent and stay on the mountain with Jesus. However, there is more to life than the mountaintop. Life is filled with peaks and valleys, and Jesus walks with us through it all. Our time on the mountain with Jesus prepares us for the valley. We are his vessels to move around in, and we share the daily experience as one.

In 1 Kings 19, God instructed Elijah, while on a mountain, to go and look for God's presence. Elijah heard God's voice eventually, but only after seeing a storm, experiencing an earthquake, and facing fire. God was not in those "big things." He made himself known in the form of a still, small voice. We often want to experience a dramatic moment with God, and then remain in the experience forever. That's not how it works. God always has something to say, but it is not always through a dramatic experience. He waits for us to ask and listen to his still, small voice. Fasting sets the stage to hear from God. And that experience, in turn, prepares us to return to the challenges of life. Are you learning to hear from God? Do you hear his still, small voice above the noise of the world and life swirling around you? It has been said that the primary ways we hear from God personally are through Scripture, the church, prayer, worship, and our circumstances. Of these, Scripture should always be primary. I pray that you seek God's voice regularly in these ways and learn to hear from him.

Discussion Questions

1. When you think of a "mountaintop" experience with God, what comes to mind? Have you had this kind of experience with God? Explain.

2. Why do you think it seems hard to find God when we are away from the mountaintop?

3. How have you learned to hear God's voice? How can you be sure it's his voice and not your own or that of the Enemy?

4. Review the primary ways we hear from God as listed in the last paragraph of this chapter. Have you heard God's voice through any of these means? Describe that experience.

5. What is your primary means for hearing God? Why do you think it would be important for Scripture to be one of our consistent means for hearing God's voice?

6. What has God's still, small voice been speaking to you lately? How will you respond?

Moses answered the people, "Do not be afraid. Stand firm and you will see the deliverance the Lord will bring you today. The Egyptians you see today you will never see again. The Lord will fight for you; you need only to be still."

—Exodus 14:13–14

34

Stand Still and I Will Fight for You

During the season of discernment and due diligence regarding the potential donation of the Sears facility, God led me and our leadership team to Exodus 14. It was an interesting passage for us because we were on the brink of receiving a miraculous blessing. Exodus 14 tells the story of Moses and the Israelites leaving Egypt and Pharaoh going back on his word and pursuing them with his entire army. Outnumbered, out of resolve, and out of options, the Israelites trembled in fear as they backed up against the Red Sea. They looked to Moses for leadership, and Moses looked to God for direction. Moses then delivered this message to the people: "Do not be afraid. Stand still, and see the salvation of the LORD, which He will accomplish for you today. For the Egyptians whom you see today, you shall see again no more forever. The LORD will fight for you, and you shall hold your peace" (Ex. 14:13–14 NKJV). These verses burned into the hearts of Overflow's leaders like a permanent brand. We knew that no matter what lay ahead, God would fight for us.

Little did we know that within a few short months we would be backed up against litigation from the mall owner and a public hearing regarding the use of our new facility as a place of worship. I found myself managing not just a church, a nonprofit organization, and a 130,000-square-foot property but also a legal and public relations battle. It was an incredibly intense time, but also one in which we saw God move on our behalf time and time again.

Before deciding whether or not to issue a permit to allow us to use our location as a church, the township planning commission held a public hearing. The hearing drew a standing-room-only crowd and regional television news coverage. During the hearing, I spoke only what had been scripted by our lawyer and spent the rest of the time praying and listening. More than 90 percent of the attendees supported our use of the facility as a church, and the planning commission ruled in our favor. God had won this battle, but there were more to come.

A short time later, we realized the township board of trustees did not intend to take the recommendation of the planning commission and was likely to deny our proposal to use the location for a church. By now our case was drawing national interest. A lawyer specializing in the Religious Land Use and Institutionalized Persons Act (RLUIPA) offered to take our case, and a representative from the RLUIPA division of the Department of Justice called as well. Despite having these incredible advocates at our disposal, we sensed that God wanted us to lay down the fight and let him lead it his way.

Within six months, the legal battle turned in favor of a new strategy, which was to sell the property rather than use it. The turning point with this new strategy came as the donor of the facility encouraged us to sell it and the judge mediating our case pushed both parties toward a sale and settlement. God had gifted us the building, and that was a great blessing. However, he then revealed that his purpose was to use this gift to provide the resources to move in another direction. We would have missed this had we not walked by faith and allowed God to reveal what he was orchestrating on our behalf through prayer, our leadership team, the donor, and the judge. God truly will speak and work through people in many different ways if we pay attention and practice discernment.

Life is full of ups and downs, including situations where we find ourselves in need of someone to fight for us. With the Sears battle, we were in one of those situations. As a three-year-old church plant with roughly one hundred people in attendance, the battle was daunting. We lacked the material resources to undertake the fight, but we had more than enough spiritual resources. This precarious position was exactly where God had led us. His first miracle had provided the means by which a second miracle could occur. It is easy to say we want God to do a miracle for us, but in order for there to be a miracle, there must first be impossible circumstances. Overflow witnessed God's miraculous provision by trusting him through not one but two impossible circumstances.

In the fall of 2009, just prior to the donation of the Sears property, I had read Exodus 14:13–14 and shared it with Overflow's leadership team. As the battle of 2010 unfolded, God had already given us his word on it. We returned to Exodus 14 and stood on the promise God had given. True to his word, God fought for us in a very unexpected way. Overflow prevailed in the situation, though not in the way we had envisioned. What fight do you find yourself in today? Are you facing a situation that seems impossible, one that calls for a miracle? Let this chapter encourage you to stand still, find peace in trusting God, and let him fight for you. Our tendency is to take things into our own hands. We fight for ourselves, and that is where we often make our greatest mistakes. I pray that you are able to experience God's peace, to be still, and to let him fight for you, whether it takes two days, two weeks, or two years.

Discussion Questions

1. What battle are you facing today that could be an opportunity to apply God's words from Exodus 14? Explain.

2. How would the belief that God is fighting for you change your approach to this situation?

3. What should you do differently with this situation in order to experience God's peace?

4. In what ways does Overflow's story of patiently allowing God to fight for them encourage you? How does it challenge you?

5. Is there any situation you have taken into your own hands that you need to let go of, lay down, or leave behind so God can fight for you?

6. What does it mean to be still and experience God's peace? In what specific ways could you do that in this season of your life?

"So he who had received five talents came and brought five other talents, saying, 'Lord, you delivered to me five talents; look, I have gained five more talents besides them.' His lord said to him, 'Well done, good and faithful servant; you were faithful over a few things, I will make you ruler over many things. Enter into the joy of your lord.'"

—Matthew 25:20–21 NKJV

35

A Mosaic of Miracles

In 2009 a leader from another community approached me, suggesting he could help start a resale store that would provide resources for Overflow Church. I was very intrigued by this idea and the potential it had to help both Overflow and our community. As I prayed about it and toured the operation in his community, I sensed God saying yes, but that the focus of our operation should be different. I felt strongly that we were to start a resale store in order to do "business as a mission." The store would be part of the nonprofit organization we were forming, which meant revenue from the store would not be used to support Overflow Church. I trusted that God would provide for both the church and the nonprofit organization. As a result, we have witnessed miracle after miracle through the resale store, known in our community as Mosaic Resale Store.

In early 2010, Christian and Stefenie Sawyer, along with their two children, relocated from Chicago to serve as founders of Mosaic Resale Store. Their faith, sacrifice, and leadership helped establish what is today a thriving ministry. The stories of God's provision for the store would make a long list, but here are just a few examples. The store held a benefit dinner at a local church that generated ten thousand dollars in start-up cash. Five churches held donation drives that generated multiple trailer-loads of goods for the store. A church from New York sent a service team to help complete the build-out of the store. A partnership with a local nonprofit led to a handful of youth summer employees sorting the donated items for sale in the store. Everyone did their part, and the store officially opened in the fall of 2010. This new business-mission was providing job training, building bridges between neighbors, and generating resources to benefit our community. It has been incredibly hard work for everyone involved, but God continues to bless the store one day at a time. We continuously seek God, offering prayer for our customers, volunteers, and employees, and for the wisdom to operate this mission according to God's plan.

Mosaic Resale Store wasn't the only place we saw stories of God's provision. They were regular occurrences for Overflow Church also, as the monthly overhead for our commercial property was more than six thousand dollars. We never missed a single payment. God was faithful and continued to weave together a mosaic of miracles. One of the greatest stories of God's provision occurred when we were eighteen months into the Sears transaction and a landlord holding prime property in a fast-growing area of our community offered Mosaic Resale Store (which is a separate 501[c3]) a five-year lease at one dollar a month. God reduced the store's overhead from some seventy-six thousand dollars per year to just twelve dollars. This allowed Mosaic Resale Store to increase their staff to over eighteen employees who were provided job training (that number is thirty-nine as of this writing). When business as mission is done by faith, God provides and an entire community is blessed.

Mosaic Resale Store was and continues to be an example of the faithful stewardship of a miracle that has touched many lives. It combines job creation, job training, discipleship, and the provision of low-cost goods to bless those in need. The store was made possible because of visionary leadership and founders with great faith and a desire to steward God's blessing to help others. In Matthew 25, Jesus told us we have been entrusted with resources we are to multiply through faithful stewardship. As we succeed, he celebrates with us and entrusts us with even more. As we steward the miracle God provides, he multiplies our effectiveness so that we can in turn truly bless others.

What are you doing with what God has given you? There are many ways to multiply his gifts, such as donating goods, volunteering time, using your spiritual gifts, and applying business skills. To do that, you must be willing to break out of your set ways of doing things. Great adventures are ahead! Take an inventory of your gifts, talents, and resources. Let God show you how to multiply the impact of those resources to be a blessing to others. What might be possible? Could you create jobs? Could you put on a dinner to raise funds for a new ministry? Is it time for you to retire from your career so you can use what you know to assist a nonprofit ministry or a church? Maybe it's time to start the business you've always dreamed of in order to be a great employer and use your business skills to help others. Whatever God is leading you to do, I pray you are encouraged to steward the miracle he wants to do in and through you. Follow him, and enjoy the ride!

Discussion Questions

1. When you read about Mosaic Resale Store's approach to "business as mission," was this a new concept for you? What benefits and challenges can you see to using the marketplace as a place of ministry?

2. Paul's vocation was a tentmaker, and Lydia was a dealer in purple dye (see Acts 16:14; 18:2–3). In what ways could your day job further the ministry of the kingdom?

3. Read Matthew 25:14–30. What does it mean to be a faithful and good steward of what God has given you?

4. What resources (time, talent, and treasure) has God entrusted to you? What are you doing with those resources?

5. What life changes could you make in order to use your life and resources to make a greater impact on the world?

6. Pray and ask God to show you the next steps in being a faithful steward and making a bigger difference in our world for him.

PART 8

Receive Rather Than Achieve

But you are the ones chosen by God, chosen for the high calling of priestly work, chosen to be a holy people, God's instruments to do his work and speak out for him, to tell others of the night-and-day difference he made for you—from nothing to something, from rejected to accepted.

—1 Peter 2:9–10 MSG

36

Little Is Much for the Chosen

Businesses as mission, or rather social enterprises, are gaining momentum and becoming quite trendy in our twenty-first-century world. These businesses exist to make money but focus on using that money to make a difference in the world. As mentioned earlier, after working as a landscape supervisor with a group of high school students in the summer of 2009, I felt a burden to continue seeing youth and young adults placed in meaningful employment. As I prayed about this for a couple of months, I couldn't shake what I was sensing from the Lord. He wanted Mosaic CCDA to start a lawn-care business. I reached out to Justin Barnes and Kyle Randall, friends from our previous church. By this time, both were serving as full-time youth pastors in new locations. Incredibly, each of them had independently sensed a stirring from God to do something different, and—get this—while mowing their own lawns had thought of creating a lawn-care company to help youth!

We talked, prayed, dreamed, and began watching God put the plan to paper, and the vision for Harbor Shine Lawn Care, a social enterprise of Mosaic CCDA, was born. In order to get this enterprise going, literally from nothing, both of these men packed up their young families and lived in the basements of Overflow Church families. The sacrifices they made and the faith they exercised were truly incredible to witness. With no direct experience and no money in the bank, we began knocking on doors in search of customers.

I believe we too often forget that when God calls us to do something, we can walk by faith and receive rather than strive to achieve. The apostle Peter put it this way: "But you are the ones chosen by God, chosen for the high calling of priestly work, chosen to be a holy people, God's instruments to do his work and speak out for him, to tell others of the night-and-day difference he made for you—from nothing to something, from rejected to accepted" (1 Pet. 2:9–10 MSG). God takes us from nothing to something, and he truly did that with Harbor Shine.

During the first summer of operation, we employed twenty young people and tended the grounds of the Harbor Shores Jack Nicklaus golf course (but not the greens!). God orchestrated this opportunity through partnerships with another local nonprofit and the golf course. In addition, we received the contract to tend the formal lawns for the Benton Harbor public schools, which had been our dream from the beginning as we wanted to put youth from the school system to meaningful work at their own schools. This contract included some fifteen residential lawns throughout our community. I will never forget sitting with the decision maker for that contract, discussing the details. At one point he looked at me and said, "Do you even have equipment?" I quickly replied, "That is the least of our worries; let's get back to the numbers." Only God could have given me that answer to respond with and helped us secure this massive contract, which allowed us to go out and get equipment. A couple of generous Christians put together some faith-based financing (given to us in great faith and with a very favorable interest rate) for us; equipment donations started coming in; and we were up and running. Today, Harbor Shine is a fully functioning business-ministry with a regional outreach. Its vision statement is "Transforming lawns and transforming lives." From nothing to something, God is truly able to provide when we walk by faith.

Many of us have memories of that moment on the playground when everyone lined up to pick teams. For many, those memories are difficult. We recall the pain of not being picked quickly or maybe not at all. For any who have felt that pain, 1 Peter 2:9–10 is a profound encouragement: God has chosen us! The ultimate team captain, the greatest coach, our God himself has chosen us to be his people and to do his work here on earth. He takes us from nothing to something, making us far more than we could ever be on our own. Harbor Shine came into being because two incredible founders joined God as he called them forward with a vision for a business-ministry. Because they chose to live on mission, this organization is now a blessing to many.

Your story may be different, but God has chosen you, too, to do great work for him. God's wants each of us to be in relationship with him and with others and to engage in the meaningful work he created us for. This fact alone should bring you great encouragement. He will take your life, whether it seems like little or much to you now, to new heights as you follow him and let him bless the work of your hands. You may not get a call from a CEO, government official, professional coach, or symphony conductor, but you have received God's call. You are chosen by him to make a difference in our world.

Discussion Questions

1. Read 1 Peter 2:9–10. What stands out to you in this passage? Why? What do you think the term *royal priesthood* means in this passage?

2. What do you think of the notion that any work done for God can be holy, not just the work of full-time Christian ministry?

3. You are chosen to be in relationship with God, in relationship with others, and engaging in the meaningful work God created for you. Which of these three do you feel you are doing well? Do you need to grow in any of these areas?

4. What is your story? Peter said we are to "to tell others of the night-and-day difference he made for you—from nothing to something, from rejected to accepted" (1 Pet. 2:9–10 MSG). With whom should you share your story today?

5. Is there anything you've considered nothing but which God might turn into something? How does Harbor Shine's story encourage you to trust God? In what ways does it challenge you?

Although the Lord gives you the bread of adversity and the water of affliction, your teachers will be hidden no more; with your own eyes you will see them. Whether you turn to the right or to the left, your ears will hear a voice behind you, saying, "This is the way; walk in it."

—Isaiah 30:20–21

37

Are You Climbing the Right Mountain?

Faith is not just trusting God for the things you want but receiving from God what he has for you. This subtle yet important difference is vital to understand. We do not place faith in ourselves or what we hope to achieve. We trust in God and what he provides for us. Nowhere has this truth been clearer to me than in the story of the Sears property, which I've referred to several times. We had miraculously received the donation of this massive facility, followed by an equally massive court battle with the owner of an adjacent property and our township board. I knew God had given us the facility, and we gladly received it. What we didn't know was the reason we had received the donation and the purpose God would eventually accomplish through it.

Too often I have been guilty of wanting to know the end at the beginning, and charging forward as if God was finished speaking into the journey. This is a common mistake by well-meaning Christians, and I wonder how much of God's abundant plan we often miss as a result. With the Sears property, we learned to let go and let God speak, and we have been blessed as a result.

Here is how the legal challenges played out. First, we cleared the hurdle with our local township planning commission. Then, we faced a judge who mediated the mall owners' lawsuit against our church. It did not take long for the mediator to recognize that their claim was solely about control of the land and their desire to eventually sell the entire mall (including our property). The mall owners needed to purchase our property for their future plans, and the judge helped them see that this was the only option rather than trying to force us out through a lawsuit. When we realized this, God's true purpose in giving us the building became clearer. We had first thought it was to be used as a single center to house Overflow Church and Mosaic CCDA under one roof. But God began to reveal other plans. While the lawsuit was being resolved, Isaiah 30:20–21 spoke clearly to me: "Although the Lord gives you the bread of adversity and the water of affliction, your teachers will be hidden no more; with your own eyes you will see them. Whether you turn to the right or to the left, your ears will hear a voice behind you, saying, 'This is the way; walk in it.'" These verses steered us to redirect our energies, and subsequent events confirmed the path ahead.

The property's donor, the late Owen "Casey" Moran, drove two hours to attend our first mediation session. Then in his mideighties, Owen pulled me aside to assure me that he had no objection to us selling the property. In fact, he recommended it. His intent was to bless our church in its mission, and he thought the sale would be a great way to accomplish that. In his words of encouragement, I heard an echo of Isaiah 30:21, "This is the way; walk in it." We could have continued stubbornly fighting for permission to use the facility, climbing the wrong mountain, but God was gracious. Though it took more than a year after that initial meeting with the judge, we were finally able to settle the dispute, sell the property, purchase a new facility that fit us perfectly, and have resources left over to accelerate the ministry of both the church and nonprofit organization.

That season of conflict was so challenging that I felt at times it would overtake me. Challenges come in different forms in all of our lives. The key to overcoming them is to determine the direction of God's leading. Maybe you are in a season of high challenge or difficulty right now, and you need direction. The challenge may be exactly what you need. God can turn the obstacle you face into a new opportunity. Also, God may want to shift your strategy or your direction, giving you a whole new approach to the challenge. Midcourse corrections seem to be God's specialty.

It is amazing how many people sense an initial direction from God and then hold so tightly to it that they don't allow him to coach them to the finish line. When you stop listening to God, you miss the real outcome he has for you. That's what we discovered through the donation of the Sears property. We knew it represented a mountain, given to us from God. We started climbing that mountain but realized we were on the wrong slope. We were to climb in a different direction—and arrive at a different destination.

God said to Abram, "Get out of your country, from your family, and from your father's house, to a land that I will show you" (Gen. 12:1 NKJV). Abram was given no details of the journey, just a direction. It took continual listening for God's direction for Abram to realize that promised destiny. Continue seeking God's guidance while you climb. At every point of challenge, listen for his direction. God will use those challenges as opportunities for growth—growth for you and for those around you. The experience will deepen your trust in him and his story—for his glory. I hope you are ready to climb the mountains God allows into your life. Let him guide every step of the journey.

Discussion Questions

1. What challenges are you facing today? Did you bring these challenges into your life, or did God bring you to them? Explain.

2. Regardless of the challenge you face, God intends to help you grow and deepen your faith through it. How does that thought encourage you? In what ways does it unsettle you?

3. What, specifically, could you do to seek God's guidance concerning this challenge during the coming week?

4. Is there any aspect of your current approach to this challenge that should be corrected immediately? Explain.

5. Is it possible that you have taken too much into your own hands or held on too tightly to your plan in this situation? What do you think prompted you to do that? What could you do, in a practical way, to surrender control to God?

6. Read Isaiah 30:20–21 and Genesis 12:1, and pray about the situation you face, asking God for guidance and direction.

"But you shall receive power when the Holy Spirit has come upon you; and you shall be witnesses to Me in Jerusalem, and in all Judea and Samaria, and to the end of the earth."

—Acts 1:8 NKJV

38

Witnesses to His Power

Christians use the terms *testimony* or *story* to describe their relationship with Jesus and how he has transformed their lives. Our stories are eyewitness accounts of the love and power of our God mediated through Jesus. Jesus said, "But you shall receive power when the Holy Spirit has come upon you; and you shall be witnesses to Me in Jerusalem, and in all Judea and Samaria, and to the end of the earth" (Acts 1:8 NKJV). Our role is to bear witness to what God has done in our world through Jesus. Beginning in late 2010, Overflow Church became a witness to God's incredible power as he transformed the life of a Muslim woman in our community.

Kareemah El-Ahmin was a lifelong Muslim, raised in a Muslim family. (To read her testimony in her own words, see the appendix of this book.) She was a well-known community leader, activist, and artist. As 2010 drew to a close, we held the first public event for our Mosaic CCDA, and Rose Hunt, our volunteer executive director, invited Kareemah to attend as her guest. From the start of the event, Kareemah experienced something different in the atmosphere, the music, the messages, and even the spirit of those attending. This intrigued her, and it opened up a conversation with Rose. Based on that conversation, the two of them decided to use the next two weeks to fast and meet at one another's apartments in the evenings to study the Bible. What boldness by Rose, what courage by Kareemah, and what a beautiful picture of what it means to be a witness to God's power!

As the two weeks drew to a close, Kareemah began to realize that if Jesus really is who he claimed to be, it would change everything about her life. One day while driving in the rain, Kareemah cried out to God, asking him to reveal his power. If Jesus is real, she prayed, make the rain stop. It stopped. Still wary, she asked God to confirm this sign in reverse. If Jesus is real, she prayed, start the rain again. It started. There on the road, Kareemah, like the apostle Paul, became a witness to God's power as Jesus supernaturally revealed himself to her.

Kareemah's experience is just one of many stories of Jesus supernaturally revealing himself to people around the globe. Many of us prayed Kareemah would have that kind of revelation during those two weeks. A few hours after Kareemah became a witness to God's power, she prayed to receive Jesus as her Lord and Savior in our church office. A few weeks later, Kareemah was baptized during a midweek service, giving witness of God's power to many. Kareemah has continued to serve as a witness by releasing her first gospel album and publishing her first book.

Kareemah's story is such a vivid reminder of God's power. He is at work in our world in miraculous ways, seeking his own. It may be tempting to read this story and think, "That's nice for her, but the life of faith in Jesus that experiences his power is not for me." That very thought is one of the greatest deceptions the Enemy has perpetuated upon Christians. We have allowed ourselves to be lulled to sleep, forgetting that we have been given the power of God to be his witnesses in the world! That power was promised in Acts 1:8 and given to believers through the Holy Spirit at Pentecost (see Acts 2), and that power continues today. As a believer in Christ, you have access to the Spirit's power. You have far more power to bear witness to God's work than you have ever realized.

Remember that when you bear witness to the power of God, you are not alone. Jesus is with you. If anything,

Kareemah's story should convince us that no one is able to convert anyone without God's power. This is God's work, and he has the power to do it. All you must do is be faithful to share your story, to tell what you know of God's work in the world and in your life. I hope you are encouraged to walk closely with God and witness about him to those around you. Don't give up on anyone; he doesn't. Don't buy the lie that any person you encounter is beyond hope or impossible to reach with the gospel. That person may be the very one God wants you to tell about his love. Empowered by the Spirit, you can simply share with others what God has done for you and what you see him doing around you today.

Discussion Questions

1. How does Kareemah's story encourage or challenge you as a witness?

2. In a practical sense, what does the power of God to witness mean? When have you experienced that power, or where have you seen it?

3. What do you see as the key to Kareemah coming to faith in Jesus Christ? How does this impact your willingness and ability to witness to others?

4. If witnessing is simply sharing with others what God has done in your life and what you see him doing in the world, what is your "witness"?

5. Is bearing witness to God's power something you feel able to do? Explain.

6. A simple approach to sharing Jesus with others is to tell what your life was like before you met Jesus, how you came to know Jesus, and what your life has been like since that time. Using that approach, how would you state your testimony in three sentences?

7. Another simple approach to witnessing is called "I3": intercede (pray for people who do not know Jesus), invest (build relationships with them), and invite (ask them to meet Jesus or come to church). Name at least three people with whom you could try the I3 approach. What will be your first step?

> The Holy Spirit testifies in every city, saying that chains and tribulations await me. But none of these things move me; nor do I count my life dear to myself, so that I may finish my race with joy, and the ministry which I received from the Lord Jesus, to testify to the gospel of the grace of God.
>
> —Acts 20:23–24 NKJV

39

True Passion Grows through "No"

By the summer of 2011, we could see the light at the end of the tunnel with the Sears property, and we ran toward it! Our sense of anticipation for a resolution to this two-year journey was high, along with the hope of moving into a new facility we had found for the church. The path behind us was marked with moments of pain and difficulty, but even that propelled us to follow Jesus with even greater passion. One significant aspect of this story was my relationship with lifelong Benton Harbor resident Tony Rolling. We had met in 2007 and, after some initial skepticism of Overflow, Tony became a good friend to Cindy and me. In fact, it was Tony who approached me with the idea of purchasing the building his church owned in Benton Harbor and he served as the broker for both parties. The property was perfect for us, and we also learned that the original owners had prayed over thirty years earlier that it would be used for a church. We were convinced this was God's work and God's timing.

To purchase the property, we needed the approval of the district board for our denomination. I had prepared a solid proposal and even met with key stakeholders prior to the meeting. When the time came to present our purchase proposal to the district board, I was convinced we had received God's favor and that theirs would follow. I could not have been more mistaken. The presentation went well until the floor was opened for discussion. Things went bad fast, and I felt I had been blindsided by a runaway train. The crucial point was that the sale of the Sears property was still pending. The board refused to allow our new property purchase until the Sears facility sale was finalized. I knew in my heart they'd made the right decision, but I still felt devastated. Despite the fact that our church staff was present at the meeting and we were to receive two awards, I left. My mood was toxic, and I knew I would say or do something I would regret. To get as far away from the situation as I could, mentally, I went to the movies.

As I took my seat in the theater just before noon — a first for me — I hoped the popcorn, soda, and the latest installment in the Captain America series would keep my mind from anything having to do with church. I was closer to burnout than I had realized, and this "No" vote from the board was a tipping point. As the movie unfolded, I found myself really enjoying the story and feeling a bit of relief. Then something unusual happened. I felt as if God was speaking directly to me through the movie dialogue. In the scene where the character Steve Rogers asks why he had been chosen to become Captain America, the researcher responds, "The serum amplifies everything that is inside, so good becomes great; bad becomes worse. This is why you were chosen. Because the strong man who has known power all his life, may lose respect for that power, but a weak man knows the value of strength, and knows . . . compassion."[1]

I started to weep, realizing that God had gone to the movies with me. He was right there in that movie theater, and he reminded me that it was because of my heart and character that he chose me, not because of my strength. Despite my weakness, God was growing me through this negative decision.

This revelation in the movie theater led to our family receiving a small grant from our denominational leaders to pursue renewal and healing at a time we desperately needed it. In complete transparency, I shared my frustrations and fears with my direct denominational leader and he responded with love and care. During the time of renewal, we took a family vacation and I took a solitude retreat at a retreat center that provided spiritual counseling and guidance. While at the retreat center I prayed, fasted, experienced sixty hours of silence and solitude, and met with a licensed Christian counselor. It was a very transformative time as I slowed down to heal, be with the Lord, and realize I was fighting for God instead of trusting that God was fighting for me. After returning to ministry truly renewed, the Sears property sold, and four months later the board said yes to purchasing the property we wanted for Overflow. Looking back, I realize that God gave me the gift of growth and healing I needed through that "No" so I would be ready for the "Yes" when it came.

Our true passion is fueled by a passionate relationship with Jesus that is initiated and sustained by him. True passion goes through—and grows through—the "No" responses we receive. In Acts 20, Paul described the brokenness and hardship he had faced and concluded, "But none of these things move me; nor do I count my life dear to myself, so that I may finish my race with joy, and the ministry which I received from the Lord Jesus, to testify to the gospel of the grace of God" (v. 24 NKJV). The phrase "But none of these things move me" is significant for anyone who is living passionately for Jesus. What does it mean to live with such clarity of purpose that you can experience hardship yet say, "None of these move me"? It means you are a person who trusts God so deeply that you can navigate the two extremes of passion: excitement and suffering.

You will be willing to live wholeheartedly for what God has called you to do. You'll throw yourself into that work with enthusiasm. But your passion will also enable you to suffer for that purpose, and even lay down your life if necessary. This latter aspect of passion is a missing element in Western Christian culture. Many have embraced the consumer values of comfort and convenience over the Christian values of suffering and sacrifice. I found that I had to walk through a very difficult situation, one I wouldn't have chosen for myself, in order to follow my passion. God often allows that. He lets us go through something difficult so we will grow and be prepared for what he has next. We can feel that the experience will break us, and it does. That's the purpose—to break the self so we can love his will. When we're passionate about what God has called us to, we can embrace seasons of suffering and growth. In retrospect, I am able to see why I had to go through the "No." I had to grow and mature in my faith through the adversity, learning to trust God's handiwork in all situations and letting go of my desire to make things happen in my strength. I had to become the person ready to receive the

"Yes" that God had just around the corner. I had to be the person that would give God both the battle and the victory, all for his glory.

Rather than giving up or running from the "No" responses in your life, embrace them as opportunities for growth and preparation. Resist the urge to move on to someone, something, or somewhere else. Instead, respond as Paul did and say, "But none of these things move me." Allow God to shape, mold, and prepare you for what he has next. As you consider the things God has called you to, realize that you will experience highs, lows, and everything in-between. May nothing move you from what he has called you to, but rather grow you for his next move!

Discussion Questions

1. What are you truly passionate about?

2. How would you define passion and its two extremes, the emotional high and the suffering low?

3. If you were to truly live with passion, what might have to change in your mind or heart?

4. Have you ever "moved" away from someone, something, or somewhere and found that your move was premature? Describe what you learned from that.

5. What celebrations or challenges are you facing today? How might God be using them to prepare you for what is next?

6. What are the lessons you will have to learn in order to move to the next season? What practical steps can you take in this season to allow God to take you deeper with him?

Note

1. "Quotes for Dr. Abraham Erskine," *Captain America: The First Avenger*, directed by Joe Johnston (Burbank: Marvel Studios, 2011), accessed April 17, 2016, http://www.imdb.com/character/ch0205341/quotes.

And do not be drunk with wine, in which is dissipation; but be filled with the Spirit, speaking to one another in psalms and hymns and spiritual songs, singing and making melody in your heart to the Lord, giving thanks always for all things to God the Father in the name of our Lord Jesus Christ, submitting to one another in the fear of God.

—Ephesians 5:18–21 NKJV

40

The Holy Spirit and What's Next

The hyper focus of American Christianity on the blessing of God, usually defined as material abundance, is a great cause for concern. The American gospel sounds more like the American Dream. Many Christians are more concerned with bigger, better, and more than we are with faith, hope, and love. Yet, according to Jesus, we are to focus on the latter and let everything else rest in God's hands. God has given us a beautiful vision for Overflow Church and our community, but it has not been an easy path or one that always resulted in the "blessings" many people seek. It has been a path of many twists, turns, triumphs, and troubles, yet it has resulted in the greatest blessing of all—the presence of God in our midst.

One key to seeing this journey through has been continuing to see God in each season. That sounds simple, but it takes intentionality to seek God morning, noon, and night; daily, weekly, monthly, and annually. As discussed previously, it was during my burnout in 2011 that I found myself in the worst condition I'd ever been, spiritually, mentally, and emotionally. This afforded me the opportunity to take a retreat to experience silence and solitude, hear from a wise Christian counselor, and have the space I needed to find Jesus and his healing. I came across 1 Peter 5:10 and felt the Holy Spirit telling me what would come next for me and Overflow. The verse says, "But may the God of all grace, who called us to His eternal glory by Christ Jesus, after you have suffered a while, perfect, establish, strengthen, and settle you" (NKJV). I knew I had suffered for a while but God was perfecting, establishing, strengthening, and settling me! That process began during the retreat and continues to this day, years later. God's process of strengthening and perfecting me is a continual one, and it happens as I ask what he has next for me, rather than me telling him what I want next.

After I returned from that life-changing retreat, God launched Overflow into a new building, new growth, new opportunities, and, more importantly, new relationships with people who would begin to follow Jesus. During that same retreat, God gave me the idea for what would become

Overflow's weekly benediction and the title of this book. The simple phrase "Go now and be the church" has become a powerful force in the life of our church and beyond it. Each week we conclude our worship service by collectively saying this benediction: "May you journey together this week, learning to passionately follow Jesus and joyfully serve others. Go now and be the church!" I cannot tell you where that vision will lead to in your life or at your church. I am not always sure where it will lead for Overflow Church! That is the exciting thing about following God's call to "Go now and be the church." Only the Holy Spirit knows what's next, and he will lead you there (see John 16:12–14).

When we begin to fully follow God and walk into the works he has prepared in advance for us, we discover how much we need him every step of the way. Paul said that we should "be filled with the Spirit" (Eph. 5:18). This does not mean one time, but constantly and continually. This ongoing saturation by the Spirit restores us, renews us, and helps us reimagine the future as God sees it. Those who dare to truly follow Jesus and take the church beyond the walls of their church building will encounter many opportunities to both laugh and lament. In the periods of laughter and joy, we soak up every moment and are fully present. In the periods of lament and brokenness, we soak in God because he is fully present.

God's wants you to trust him as you go now and be the church in ways that will stretch you and require you to be filled with the Spirit. He is your only hope for what is next (see Rom. 15:13). The beauty of this relationship with God cannot be overstated. You will not be alone as you follow his plans, and you do not have to rely on your own strength when you are weak. He will supply it! If you are in a period of suffering and brokenness now, turn to him for restoration, strength, and peace. He is able and faithful to provide it.

As you are restored, strengthened, and settled, you will be able to help others. God is writing a beautiful story in our world, and you are part of it. As you participate in God's story of restoration, redemption, and renewal, you have the privilege of inviting others into it. Nothing you suffer is wasted in this process. How can you know what is next? Seek him, listen, and obey the leading of his Spirit. Start with prayer, Bible reading, and Sabbath observance, and then dive deeper into the spiritual disciplines of solitude and silence. God is ready to take you to the next level if you will make the time and space for him in your life. The Holy Spirit knows what is next for you, and he will lead you to passionately go now and be the church.

Discussion Questions

1. In what areas of your life do you feel as if you've suffered for a while? Describe that experience.

2. In what ways are you seeking to let God restore, strengthen, and settle you for what he has next?

3. What spiritual disciplines (such as prayer, Bible reading, Sabbath observance, silence, and solitude) do you currently practice? Which disciplines would you like to acquire? Why?

4. What could you do to explore these disciplines as pathways to renewal and strengthening for what's next in your life?

5. What thoughts or questions does the idea of being constantly and continually filled by the Holy Spirit trigger for you? With whom could you discuss these?

6. As you consider what is next for you and your church, what role do you see the Holy Spirit playing? How can you share this insight with others?

7. What are your next steps in continuing to be the person God has created you to be so that you can do his works?

8. With whom will you share your passion to go now and be the church? When will you do it?

APPENDIX

Overflow Stories
2007–2014

Dalynn Holling
Schools of Hope

Note: Schools of Hope was a ministry of the Overflow Christian Community Development Association (now known as Mosiac CCDA) that provided an afterschool literacy intervention program for students in grades 1–3 in the Benton Harbor public schools from 2011–2013. Schools of Hope's story, and my story in it, is about God's perfect timing and our need to wait on him until the time is right.

In the spring of 2010, I applied to be on a church plant team through my university. My heart has always sought adventure and to be right where God wants me to be, but as the reality of another summer away from home and the fears of the unknown started to sink in, I began to have my doubts. Someone from the university reached out to encourage me and shared some of Overflow Church's mission and Pastor Brian's heart to see a literacy program brought to the area. I immediately felt God tugging at my heart to join him and be a part of this movement. Little did I know the journey I was about to embark on.

After spending three months in the Benton Harbor/ St. Joseph community, I fell in love with the people, their stories, and Overflow's desire to see reconciliation. The following spring, after graduating, I felt God pulling me back to this church and community.

I spent that summer praying and seeking God's will for my life. In September I packed up my belongings and headed to the Benton Harbor/St. Joseph area, confident that this was where God wanted me. I worked quickly to get licensed as a substitute teacher so I could start making ends meet in this "real world" that I had just been thrust into. I began to hear about Schools of Hope and how this dream was about to become a reality but, at that point in my life, I brushed off being a part of it. I was excited it was happening and I would be able to witness it, but I was again bogged down by the unknowns and financial worries. God wasn't having it, though. He once again began to tug at my heart, reminding me of my passion for children and literacy and stirring up a holy discontent about the extreme need for this program in the community. When Brian approached me about being the assistant teacher that winter, I trusted God and took the leap.

As a result of churches coming together to do kingdom work, we are impacting kids' lives for good. I've seen God working in our students' lives, in their families, in the school, and in building bridges in the community. It has been an amazing experience watching God, in his perfect timing, orchestrate all of this according to his plan.

Pastor Sam and Rebecca Maddox: Going Above and Beyond to Support the Kingdom

My wife, Rebecca, and I planted Light and Life Wesleyan Church in July 2003 and contacted Brian Bennett in 2007 about how our church could get involved with Overflow. Brian and Cindy were experiencing what we were experiencing (as new church planters in southwest Michigan). We had to get involved because the stories (in most church plants) of church planting are miraculous.

I shared my desire to support Overflow Church with the key leadership at our church and then with the congregation. Our congregation knows well my dislike for onions, which stems from bad experiences with them during childhood. At our church dinners, people inform me if a dish contains onions. Even so, I announced that I believed so much in what was happening at Overflow that I would eat onions to raise funds! Our treasurer responded, "I'll give a hundred bucks to see that!"

I asked Brian and Cindy to come share their vision at our annual picnic. After worship, we enjoyed our afternoon meal, and cameras were ready to record my once-in-a-life-time meal of onions. Thanks to the Internet, our district superintendent, Mark Gorveatte, heard of our stunt while traveling in New Zealand!

People can give to church planting in different ways, and my little effort motivated our church to help canvass neighborhoods in Benton Harbor, pray, and provide teaching. Overflow has been encouraged, and we have too. Brian and Cindy have a set of opportunities and challenges unique to Benton Harbor. We were blessed by helping to get the word out and gather workers in a fun way. I don't want any more onions, but I am willing to get out of my comfort zone for Jesus and the many he is reaching through church planting. We care because Jesus cares!

Mark Thomas: Seeds of Change

My wife and I were part of the Overflow Church launch team and have been here since the beginning. We were both members of another church but felt it was not doing enough to go after the unchurched and the de-churched. It was a great church with a great group of people; anyone would do anything to help others within the church. But it was getting older and not attracting new or young families, and I felt we needed to have a more contemporary service in order to attract the young families and the unchurched. I was met with resistance at every turn.

My daughter, who knew what I was trying to accomplish, lived in Holland, Michigan, at the time and heard Brian speak at her church about his vision for a church in West Michigan. She gave Brian my number, and he called. We met at 10:30 p.m. at a restaurant, and Brian told my wife and me about how he wanted to build a church that crossed boundaries and wanted to reach the unchurched and de-churched.

Although it was very difficult to leave our former church, we loved what we heard from Brian and were on board. I love it when Brian tells how many people at Overflow have accepted Christ and been baptized. The great news is not only that Overflow has reached the unchurched but also that the seeds I planted at my previous church grew. They eventually started a contemporary service and are also reaching new young families. You never know what God has planned or when and where the seeds you plant will grow.

Chris Craig: Watching God's Story Unfold

I was new to Overflow Church when, because of my background (with church leadership, business, construction, and finance), I was asked to become involved with our newly donated property, the Sears facility. Joining the team, I saw the excitement and faith present and the ministry potential that this property could provide. At the same time, I was very much concerned about the overhead that this property would demand from this fledgling congregation. Being new to both the team and the church, I felt that for the time being I would be silent on this issue and see how it played out. We went ahead with some preliminary plans to help figure out what it would cost to retrofit this building for our intended use.

About this time, we received a cease and desist order from the town. This began what would be a lengthy two-year legal process that would test everyone's faith and resolve. The pressures on the pastor were enormous during this period — but God had a plan. God knew that the true value of this property was not as a church but as an asset.

First, God protected us financially in miraculous ways. Through this two-year process, the people who donated the property to us decided to pick up all expenses related to the facility. I had never encountered this in my professional life. It was a blessing that could only have been given by believers.

Second, God planted a seed. What if we sold this property and used the proceeds to purchase a different one? Along with this notion came the news that the mall associated with this property wanted to buy the Sears facility! Only in God's timing.

So our search began and culminated in purchasing the property we now call home. We could not have asked for a more perfect location to fulfill God's vision for Overflow Church, a church for all people. In addition to this, it was a fulfillment of another pastor's prayer for this location over thirty years earlier.

Only God can orchestrate a story like this. He protected us from a situation that would have been way too costly to afford and gave us the perfect home at the perfect location. It is a privilege to be part of it.

Randy Willis: Holy Discontent

In July 2007, I found myself in the middle of a pastoral change at the church I was attending. I felt the need for a change from the comfort of a suburban church. I had previously served at an inner-city church in Grand Rapids and had found a sense of purpose and satisfaction in that.

Someone from the West Michigan district of The Wesleyan Church told me about Brian Bennett and his desire to plant a church in Benton Harbor area. I had worked in the area a few times in connection with my job and had this sense that I needed to check it out. I got Brian's name and contact information. We met, and I heard his heart and vision.

But my wife needed convincing. We wanted our daughter to graduate from high school before we considered relocating. Once graduation was over, we put our house up for sale and started the long process of selling a home during the down market of 2008.

We finally sold our home after fifteen months, during which we had commuted back and forth. However, our home sold for a fraction of its worth and we lost fifteen years' worth of equity. When we moved to Benton Harbor, we had only enough money for a down payment and to buy some appliances for the new house.

I remember hanging out at the Overflow office in the mall during the early days, dreaming of what a new movement would look like. We started with small groups of people and Bible studies. Some have stayed, and some have moved on. We have traveled through the transitions from the mall, to the theater, and now to our new home on Napier Avenue.

I started with the church as the outreach director but felt the "holy discontent" to use my gifts as a photographer in the school system. I have now started a ministry with the sports teams in the school system, which enables me to funnel kids into the youth group at church where my wife and I serve as leaders.

Carolyn O'Connor: Unexpected Endings

In the fall of 2007, I drove up to the Orchards Mall in Benton Harbor—an eager graduate student with visions of ministry and seeing this Overflow church plant. This was my first "real world" class project and, like many students, I was convinced there was something I could do to help. The truth is, Overflow has taught me more than I have been able to "help." When I did that project, I had no idea that six years later I'd be working full time at Overflow. It wasn't in my vision or plan. Yet, God's plan and purpose were so much better than my limited dreams. Isaiah 55:8 says, "'For My thoughts are not your thoughts, neither are your ways My ways,' says the LORD" (NKJV). So much of what has happened at Overflow (and paralleled in my own life) has held true to that verse. Looking back, the prayers that were prayed in those early days are coming to fruition now, and God was preparing us then for what he wanted to do now and in the future. It wasn't easy by any stretch of the imagination, and there have been sacrifices made along the way that only God knows. The journey on God's path was never promised to be simple or easy, but it is worth every test, trial, burden, pain, and ache because God's process brings out the best and fashions us to be more like him.

Overflow has endured much over the years, but it continues to thrive because it allows God to clear away the things that would distract from the mission and vision that God has for it. When I drove up in 2007 (for a short-term assignment) and came in 2008 (to join the Overflow Church leadership team), I had no idea what lay before me and what the years would bring, but looking back, I would not trade one minute. God continues to shape me and develop me as he has done with Overflow, and I hope that he will say to both me and the people of Overflow, "Well done, my good and faithful servant."

Sharon and Marvin Henderson: God's Plan and Timing

Before we came to Overflow, Marvin was unchurched and I was de-churched. We both came with gaping spiritual holes that were too large for us to fill. Our marriage was broken, and other relationships were in complete disrepair. I had practically given up on going to church and giving my heart to anything. But God had other plans!

Mark and Cathy Ficks, whom Marvin had met at an estate sale, where he bought an item worth five dollars, invited him to Overflow. Mark and Cathy told Marvin that if he came to their church on Sunday, they would reimburse him for his purchase. He did not take them seriously.

Fast forward to late summer. My kids had been riding their bikes and started talking to someone named Cindy, who I thought was a child. I soon figured out that Cindy was not a child but a white woman. My husband and I walked to her house, which was at the other end of the block, to meet this woman who was talking to my children. I learned that Brian and Cindy were pastors, and they invited us to their church. We came home and talked about going back to church, but we still did not act upon this invitation. Following that encounter, we visited one other church before we visited Overflow.

The day we went to Overflow Church changed my life forever. My view of God and his kingdom was expanded that day. I don't remember what the sermon was about or who was there, but the one thing I'll never forget is how everyone wrapped their arms around us. When we came through those theater doors, people smiled and really noticed us, and from all accounts cared about us. I saw the kingdom in action for the first time in a long time. What we learned was that God's plan and timing are never what we expect but always what we need (see Jer. 29:11).

Kareemah El-Amin: From Islam to Christ

My conversion on November 17, 2010, was nothing short of miraculous, because I truly believed that faith in Islam was the only way to ensure my place in heaven, something that had always been a deep longing and desire. I had no frame of reference to change my faith; however, I did have an earnest desire to go to heaven, and I believe God answered my prayer because he knew my heart was sincere even though I was not a Christian. His grace and mercy know no bounds, and, yes, God loves Muslims too!

Going to Overflow, a predominately white church with a young white pastor, was another miracle in itself. I, like many, feel the pull to be connected to people with whom I share cultural, experiential, and historical backgrounds. Yet I know being called to Overflow was God's way of drawing me into a destiny that would allow me to become a bridge builder, reconciler, and voice for a true reflection of the body of Christ.

Overflow embodies Christ in his fullness through a myriad of colors, cultures, textures, nuances, and experiences all designed to reflect the world and community in which it lives, interacts, and serves. Overflow's history speaks to the voice of Christ in each of us, calling us out of our traditions, comfort, routine, and religion while calling us into a deeper, richer, and more intimate relationship with Christ through one another. In 2010 I, a lifelong Muslim, accepted Jesus Christ as my Lord and Savior.

Gary Bennett: Prayer and Peace

We gathered at the community center, the one near the old Sears property at the Orchards Mall. Our mission was to launch the ministry of Overflow Church with a prayer walk and times of prayer while driving in the community of Benton Harbor.

Before we set out, we had a brief time of worship and prayer together, then Pastor Brian gave instructions and handed out maps of the city explaining the various locations he wanted us to go to and offer prayer. This was a strategic movement to cover the area and its people with prayer, and to prayerfully cover the humble beginnings of Overflow Church.

While it was not originally planned, I volunteered to stay back and take care of baby Dawson. I asked for his stroller, saying that he and I would do a prayer stroll of the mall and its stores, that Papa and grandson would cover this market-place with prayer! It was agreed; and with a bottle of nour-ishment, a few dry diapers, his trusty pacifier, and favorite blanket, we started walking.

Dawson and I slowly covered the mall, praying throughout for the next couple of hours. There were times when I knew my little grandson was in tune with the Holy Spirit as I prayed. Sometimes I would stop and sit on a bench, and Dawson would cease his activity in the stroller and listen to me softly and fervently pray. I was blessed, and I know that together we touched the heavenly throne regarding that marketplace.

There were also a few moments when my grandson was not in tune, and I finally realized he needed to take different action. After a bottle, a few good burps, and a much-needed diaper change, he settled down and we continued our prayer stroll.

As we walked through store after store, I silently prayed for the employees and customers, and Dawson fell asleep.

His level of contentment and complete trust was second to none. His peaceful sleep spoke to me in a way that I did not expect. It reminded me of Jesus, when he was fast asleep in the back of a boat during a tumultuous storm while his disciples were having panic attacks. Jesus' peaceful contentment and complete trust in the heavenly Father allowed him to sleep soundly (see Mark 4:35–41).

I began to claim that peace and trust for Overflow Church, for the church to have an intimate understanding that our heavenly Father is in control and there is nothing for us to fear, and for the body and every believer to develop a level of complete trust, which is steady and unshakable, always trusting the Lord regardless of circumstances. Dawson was so young that he will never recall the prayer stroll that we took that first year. But I know that our prayer time together will remain memorable for me, and effectual for the kingdom work of Overflow Church in the Benton Harbor area.

Now Dawson has become a prayer warrior in a child's body. He will stop and pray, prompted by the Spirit, in a store, on the street, in the yard, or wherever needed. When he prays, the words are spoken with such power that they go beyond his young frame to the throne to accomplish much in the spiritual realm.